The
JAR
SPELLS
Compendium

2023 Edition

Unleash your Magic with the Power of Witch Bottles
and Master the Art of Witchcraft.
Includes 120+ Spell Recipes for Love, Protection,
Wealth, Healing, Luck, and More

HANNAH
DIXON

ISBN: 979-8357680792
10 9 8 7 6 5 4 3 2 1

DOWNLOAD YOUR BONUS NOW:
2 FREE eBooks

Witchcraft for Beginners

Wicca for Beginners

The bonus is **100% FREE.**
You don't need to enter any details except your name and email address.

To download your bonus scan the QR code below or go to

https://books-bonuses.com/hannah-dixon-bonuses

Table of Contents

4

Introduction

What Is Witchcraft?

Witchcraft is the art of using willpower to manifest and live one's ideal life. Witchcraft will be referred to as a path because the path leads to healing, happiness, and eventually enlightenment.

As a result, creating a single path for everyone to follow might be challenging because we all come from diverse places and have different needs and desires. However, there are a few simple witchcraft ways that may appeal to us:

- Light magic promotes happiness and love.
- Dark magic is a type of magic that employs hexes, curses, and malice.
- Energetic work: Using the universe's energy, such as crystals, for healing purposes.
- Spirit/ancestor work: Working with the practitioner's ancestors and spirits.
- Devotional: Developing a practice centered on a deity's devotion.

History of Witchcraft

From the term "Wicca," Witch means "wise one." Witches were revered in Antiquity and remained so until the Christian era. Christian clerics began to stalk and prohibit them because of their differing views. The Inquisition was the most potent weapon against witches; we no longer approve of it. Witchcraft is emerging from the shadows in current times, and the true nature of witchcraft believes in the essence of all things working in harmony. Witchcraft isn't evil, and it has nothing to do with the devil. Witches who worship the devil are vulnerable to black magic.

Witches and wizards were sought after by those who truly understood witchcraft for their potent spells and assistance with daily tasks. The Inquisition offered examples of witches using black magic, flying, killing other people, and taming black wolves to have a justification to persecute them. They were charged with establishing satanic pacts. It is untrue, as most witches do not believe in the devil. As a future witch, you should know the difference between white and black magic. The dread of humans, when confronted with odd things, is demonstrated by the Crusades against witchcraft. The Inquisition employed witchcraft as a punishment and fear-inducing tool. That is why witchcraft is regarded in such a negative light. Because of the Inquisition, most of our forefathers kept their faith and way hidden.

People who have a good understanding of witches are the ones who can debunk this myth. If you want to be a witch, you should understand everything you can about the burning times and the misconceptions of a delusional and unfair era. Because this is your past, you must be able to dispel prevalent myths. You're on a quest for knowledge, and what you're looking for is right around the corner on this book page.

Those who practice witchcraft regard it as a religion. Witches believe in the existence of God and Goddess. Witches believe that all things, including themselves, possess the God and Goddess's energy. Most witches consider themselves people of the soil because of their deep belief in nature.

The Celts were the first to practice witchcraft. The Celts were devout Christians who worshipped both God and Goddess. They saw a "Divine Creator" in everything of nature. Reincarnation was thought to occur after death, with the deceased journeying to the "Summer Land" to rest before being reborn.

Paganism is the name given to the Celts' beliefs and customs. The word pagan comes from the Latin word magus, which means "country dweller." it stemmed from the Celts' passion for the land and the natural world. Druids, "understanding the oak tree," were the Celts' "priests. The pagans' beliefs and practices expanded to include making healing potions and ointments, casting spells, and performing magical acts. Witchcraft is used to describe all of this.

Before the 14th century, witchcraft was seen as a religion, including healing rituals. Divination and fortune-telling are practiced. People with various religious beliefs and rituals were suspicious of witchcraft and labeled it demon worship. It's simply a case of people being afraid of what they don't know. Witchcraft predates Christianity, and there are no "bad" beings in the witchcraft religion. Witches believe in nature's harmony and the divine energy of the gods and goddesses, which should be present in all living and nonliving things.

Witchcraft has a tumultuous past, with witches being punished for their beliefs throughout history. Christians have long been the primary source of the concept that witches are bad people who worship the devil. Witch hunts have been documented on various occasions. Witches were persecuted in what is now the Old Testament of the Bible around 560 B.C. Around 420, St. Augustine spoke against witchcraft, claiming it was impossible. Witchcraft trials began in the mid-1400s. Witches and those who practiced witchcraft were frequently tortured.

Over 1000 people were executed for witchcraft accusations in the early 1500s. King James of Scotland authorized the torture and persecution of witches in 1591. A giant witch hunt in the history of France took place in the 1640s, after which witch-hunting began to decline. The Last Witch in England was put to death in 1682. Perhaps the most well-known executions were those that took place during the Salem Witch Trials in 1692. Over 1000 people were executed for witchcraft accusations in the early 1500s. King James of Scotland authorized the torture and persecution of witches in 1591. A giant witch hunt in the history of France took place in the 1640s, after which witch-hunting began to decline.

Even though witchcraft and those who practice it have been condemned for centuries, many individuals still engage in it today. Today, between 750,000 and 5,000,000 people practice witchcraft in some way. It is thought to be a fast-growing religion.

Witchcraft Today

Old Wicca (sometimes called "the old ways") refers to the traditions and practices set by Gerald Gardner, as well as those set by Alex Sanders (1926–1988), who brought the Gardnerian tradition to the United States in the 1960s. Back then, the terms Wicca and witchcraft were considered synonymous, which isn't the case today.

In the past, the only way to become Wiccan or learn about the craft was through rigorous training and initiation into one of the traditions, such as Gardnerian, Alexandrian, Dianic, Saxon, Celtic, or other Church of Wicca movements. Old Wicca was considered secretive and selective of its members. Many covens were created by former coven initiates; to become a High Priest or Priestess, you had to be a part of the coven for many years, studying and learning everything you could.

The works of Scott Cunningham (1956–1993) were the turning point in providing accessible information to the public about Wicca. Cunningham wrote more than 50 books, several of which were about magic, Wicca, and solo magical practice. Cunningham's books provided a new way of practicing Wicca that didn't require a coven initiation. In the past, if you wanted to find information on Wicca, you had to learn from the teachings of coven members as an initiate.

But Cunningham believed that there shouldn't be secrets besides the ones a practitioner kept in their own practice. Cunningham tried being part of covens but opted for solo practice, and wanted to share his knowledge with anyone who had an interest. This accessibility helped Wicca evolve into Neo-Wicca, which much of the practice consists of today.

Modern Wicca includes newer Wiccan traditions inspired by Old Wicca. Many practices of Old Wicca are still
present in Modern Wicca, including incorporating the masculine and feminine aspects of divinity and performing rituals for holidays, phases of the moon, equinoxes and solstices, the elements, initiations, and other important life phases.

Wicca changes and adapts with the times, but its core values and beliefs remain the same—honoring nature, the seasons or Sabbats, divinity, and practicing ethics. Modern Wicca is eclectic in nature, meaning that it derives from different ideas and diverse sources. Wicca today is considered amorphous and can easily have roots in various beliefs or practices. My practice, for example, consists of Wicca and witchcraft that encompass astrology, tarot, herbalism, and spirit work. All you have to do is follow your heart to the path that's right for you.

Witchcraft Fundamentals

A spell refers to a magical formulation that is normally intended to trigger a magic effect on either a person or an object. The spells are normally created through the chanting of a series of words, singing, or even mere speaking. The series of words are known to have magical powers, and a person or object under a particular spell has their actions and thoughts dictated by the specification of said spell. Usually, the spells are cast by witches or groups of persons who believe in their powers, and they are believed to cause instantaneous reactions. Creating your own Wiccan spells is actually simpler than believed to be. While most witches and spell casters usually use ancient spells created by other people, there are times when they want to use customized and specific spells. In this case, the writing of individual spells is imminent.

It all depends on your preference, if you want to perform spells or not, either way, it is not compulsory to do spells and magic to be Wiccan. Further, if you want to create or do spells, remember the crede "Harm None" as this is an essential part of Wicca. It doesn't mean that if you perform spells, you can destroy your enemies this is NOT true! If this is your motive for becoming a Wicca, then I suggest you stop reading this book as it won't get you near your goal. So, I repeat, the practice of Wicca is to commune with nature and to open the realm of the gods and goddesses to be one with them through connecting with nature.

When it comes to witchcraft, making a spell is easy it's just like creating a new home-cooked meal recipe; but of course, it requires practice. So, let's just stick to how spells are generally done.

Your Purpose

The first step in doing a spell is to know the purpose of the spell. The goal has to be specific. For example, if you are looking for love, a love spell won't do the trick because are you already eyeing someone. Or maybe you want an ex to come back to you? Or maybe you still need to meet that special someone. This is how specific your purpose should be.

Materials

The next step is finding the 'perfect' spell and gathering all the necessary materials to do the spell. You can also make your spell by making use of 'correspondences' as these are lists of items with their corresponding purposes. Take for example you can use the herb Damiana which corresponds to lust and love. To make a spell, would need around 2 to 5 items are sufficient. You can also make use of crystals or candles and work with colors too.

Words

When casting a spell, using words best helps you to focus your intention and energy. Some spells already have words included. But if you are making your own spell, then you have to be creative when it comes to creating chants.

Timing

Although this is not as important as other steps in casting a spell, with the right timing, it can add additional power to your spell. For a little magical boost, you can pick the right phase of the moon or the right day of the week. Check out some correspondence tables to boost the power of your spell.

Put It All Together

Many people believe that just chanting the words of a spell and going through the motions will lead to a successful spell. But in reality, what makes a good spell powerful and successful depends on your focus. You have to focus on what you are doing and you have to take your time. Thus, it means you need to learn the spell before you begin. You also need to visualize the energy and your intentions as vividly as you can and this is the hardest part when casting spells because it takes practice and experience.

All You Need To Prepare Spells

In the practice and observance of nearly every religion, there are sacred objects that are incorporated into that religion. It can be in the form of chalices, amulets, candles, shrines with statues of deities to be worshipped, or special clothing worn by the officiants of the religious ceremonies.

People like to create and use tools or artifacts in their sacred rituals to create and keep a focus on the spiritual energy in the rituals of their practices.

Wicca is no exception, using many tools in their rituals that all have a specific placement on the altar, a particular use, and a symbolic significance.

The tools are used to create a focus on the spiritual energy and to direct it to make a direct connection with the spirit world. There is, however, an important but subtle distinction between the use of symbolic objects by other religions and the use of them by Wiccans.

The difference is that Wiccans recognize the fact that they share in nature's powers as co-creators in the power that is given by the Goddess and the God and they are not subject completely to the will and calling of the higher power.

The tools used by Wiccans are both practical and symbolic because each action and each object used and performed in the circle of sacred energy is intended deliberately to direct and harness this force of co-creativity.

The tools are used to protect the person and the ritual against unwanted influences of forces of energy, to perform spell work and other works of magic, and to welcome and invoke the energies of the Elements and of the deities. The tools themselves have no powers of magic and only work to conduct the personal power of the follower who is using them.

There is no exact set of ritual tools since the tools that are needed will vary depending on the intended use and the tradition. Some solitaries and covens will use a diverse range of objects to observe highly elaborate rituals, while other people and covens will want to keep things more simplified and will use a few tools for multiple functions in the ritual.

The tools most commonly thought of as necessities in the practice of Wicca are the censer which is used to hold incense, the athame (a-tha-may) which is the knife used in rituals, the pentacle, the wand, the chalice or cup, and the candle or candle the follower wishes to use. A few other tools that are often mentioned and sometimes used include the ritual scourge, the staff, the sword, the bell, the cauldron, and the broom. It is also considered useful though not mandatory to have altar cloths and decorations, herbs and crystals, a plate for offerings or ritual food, a boline which is a special knife for carving and cutting, and images of the Goddess and God.

It is not necessary to compile all of these articles in order to begin your practice. The best way is to begin small and gather your tools one or two at a time until you have collected all of the ones you feel you need. There will be some that you will not ever feel a need to own.

And while it is nice to go out and buy all brand-new items, it is totally not necessary. Some of the items that you need to collect may already be in your possession being used for other purposes or hidden away in a closet or cabinet.

A special or unique goblet or cup that you already own and that has special meaning to you can become your chalice. You can buy items through online shops, but it is also fun to visit resale or second-hand shops where you can feel and touch each piece to see if it sends you a particular feeling or energy. If you are artistically inclined, you might be able to make your own tools.

Or you may be able to find things in nature that might be used as a tool on your altar. A clean, sterile clamshell that has been cleansed could be an amazing chalice, and a lovely small stick from a special bush or tree can be a great wand. Another way to gather your objects is to create and send out an intention for them and be receptive to their arrival. Do not be impatient in your search but do be receptive to seeing the possibilities in things you see in your everyday life.

Don't forget to record in your book what you acquired and when you acquired as tool gathering is an important step in your Wiccan journey.

No matter where or how you find your tools if it is most important that you take the time to cleanse your tools of any unwanted residual energy they may have picked up in their previous environments and to consecrate the tools for the purpose of your practice of rituals. Even though some tools are purchased new and are promised to have a special consecration, it is still preferred that you cleanse them and instill them with your own energy. Once the tools are cleansed and consecrated it is best to store them in their own private place where they can keep their energy safe and not mix it in with the everyday objects that are in your life.

To begin your collection many Wiccans believe it is important to have one tool that represents each of the Elements. You would need to gather an athame for Fire, a wand for Air, a chalice for Water, and a pentacle to represent Earth although you could also use a nice bowl of sea salt. The important thing is that you will feel a special connection and energy to each of the items that you have chosen. So if a particular tool just doesn't feel right, do not use it. Even though there is a good bit of physical activity in the practice of Wicca, all of the power lies in the energetic connection that the follower has with the divine and the spiritual world.

The Altar

The altar might need to do more than one function in your homes, such as acting as a desk or a table, or it might be its own dedicated piece of furniture. Its only real need is that it has a flat top for ceremonial use. It is preferred that the altar is made of a natural material like wood or stone.

Any physical object that you have charged with magical energy will be suitable for use as an altar that will contribute to the work of the ritual. If you are performing spell work or rituals outside then try to find an old stump of a tree or a large rock in order to get as close to nature as possible.

Decorate the altar by using colored fabric or scarves. This method will work particularly well if you find yourself using an everyday piece of furniture of a natural object outdoors. Many Wiccans prefer to follow the colors of the season when putting decorations on their altars, so they might use petals from flowers during the celebration of Spring or holly berries and fir tree sprigs during the season of Yule. Images of deities and crystals and stones are also fine to add as long as you leave the room needed for the tools you will be using.

When you place the tools on the altar there are several ways to lay them out according to the ritual that is being performed. They will also vary according to the various traditions, but there will be some characteristics. One of the types of layouts will divide the altar into two halves. All of the tools will be placed on the left side and will be associated with the Elements of Water and Earth and the Goddess as these are considered to be her Elements.

The right side of the altar will be devoted to the Elements of Air, Fire, and God. Another way to lay the altar out is to place the representations of the Goddess and the God in the center of the altar and put the remainder of the tools around them according to the four directions and the Elements. In this method, the tools that are associated with Fire will face South, and the tools that are associated with the Earth will face the North direction.

No matter what tradition you might be following set up the altar to suit your individual tastes and space restrictions. Some people will prefer an elaborate altar arrangement following a specific pattern, and some people will prefer to follow a more eclectic version that uses patterns that resonate with their own individual energy patterns. In addition, while it is nice to have a dedicated space in which to do rituals the kitchen table will work just fine if space is a consideration.

The Athame

This is one of the primary tools for the Wiccan altar. The athame resides in the East which is the direction that represents choice, thought, and mind. It can be made of carved stone, wood, or metal since it is not a knife that is used but rather a symbolic symbol. The Athame holds the God or yang energy. They are used to direct energy that is needed for recalling and casting rituals. They are not used to cut any item on the physical plane.

The Bell

The Bell is used to represent the Voice of the Goddess. If you ring the Bell during the ritual it will bring the attention of the Divine to you and will focus your attention on the Divine. The Bell can be used to call healing energy to you and to clear away any unwanted energy. This is especially useful at the end of a ritual or spell casting but can be done at any time.

The Candle

The altar will commonly hold four candles that are color-coded and stand for each of the four directions. They will be set in the direction they are representing. Blue or aqua is used for the West, orange or red candles stand for the South, white or yellow for the East, and brown, green, or black for the North. If no Goddess or God candles are being used then the center will have candles that are gold, silver, or white. Candles are used to call and hold the Powers that lie in each direction.

When the Goddess or God candles are used they ate set in the center of the altar or on either side of the Pentacle. Another option is to use a large pillar type of candle to represent the Goddess or to use the three candles to represent the Crone, the mother, and the Maiden which are black, red, and white. The energy of the Divine will be invoked by using these candles.

The Chalice

The chalice represents the Mother Goddess and is one of the most important tools on the Wiccan altar. Any wine-style glass or cup will do just fine, or a fancy ornate version may be used. The only qualifications are that the vessel is curvy or round and holds water. The chalice will be placed on the West side of the altar which is the direction of Water. The chalice will be used for the drink offering in the ceremony, to hold the salt water concoction, or to offer a drink to the Divine.

The Deities

It is always a welcome addition to any altar to have representations or images of the goddesses and gods that are special to you even though these are not technically considered to be tools of the altar. These are there to remind you of the Divinity and they can actually hold energy and vibrations of the Divine. The Divine will dwell on this living temple that your altar has become.

The Plate

Some sort of vessel in which to place offerings to the goddesses and gods will go directly to the center of the altar. This can be in the form of a cup, bowl, or a small dish or plate. If needed the cauldron or chalice may be used for the plate until a suitable plate can be acquired. When the ceremony is finished the offerings will be placed into some form of live water like a lake or a river or buried or poured into the Earth in order to send them to the Divine.

The Offerings

You will bring to the altar the things you will use to honor the Divine such as a prayer or a small gift. Anything that is beautiful to you can be used as an offering, such as keeping live flowers on the altar. The offering should not be anything that will bring harm to any living entity because anything that you cause harm to will cause harm to the Divine since the Divine lives in all things. And since the offerings will be returned to the Divine they should not be things that will harm or have been harmed.

The Pentacle

This five-point star inside of a circle is placed in the center of the altar and serves to offer power and protection to your work in magic.

The Wand

This is just a portable version of the broom. It can be made out of any material that is naturally occurring in nature. Wood is the preferred medium for a wand because wood is naturally occurring in nature and is easy to find and use. The wand is used for channeling magical energy and for divination. In the place of the athame, they can be used to recall and cast circles. On the altar, the wand goes in the South because it represents God, or energy and the transformation and power or magic and will.

The Broom

The broom is not actually an altar tool and would not fit on top of the altar but is nice to have it nearby to cleanse the sacred space around the altar.

The Cauldron

A cauldron is a three-legged cast-iron pot used for cooking. Cauldrons are made in all sizes from tiny to huge. They are great for burning things like herbs or incense. The cauldron is one of the most common tools to put on the altar. To create a very uniquely Pagan-inspired incense, place an incense charcoal into the cauldron, cover it with powders or herbs, and light it with fire. Just use caution when burning things anywhere. The legs of the cast iron cauldron will generally keep the heat from reaching what the cauldron is standing on but it never hurts to have some sort of fireproof trivet underneath just in case. The cauldron can also be used to hold brews like complex spells or simple saltwater purifications.

Crystal Ball

This tool is used to represent the Goddess. Wiccans gaze into their crystal ball to have a vision. You can find crystal balls in different sizes and types. However, once you acquire a crystal ball, make sure that you charge it magically as soon as you can. Crystal balls have long been used in witchcraft and other similar practices.

Sensor

This tool is used to hold the incense that you burn during your rituals. You can find sensors in different sizes, shapes, and materials. They are typically made of brass. Nonetheless, you may also use a hanging sensor or a glass tray if it is more convenient for you. A hanging sensor is actually ideal if you wish to disperse the smoke from your incense during your ritual sessions.

Altar Tile

This tool is used as the central area during the ritual process and may contain a pentagram. It is available in different materials. Your altar tile can be of any size, but it is better to have one that fits your altar perfectly. You can also choose to have symbols engraved on it if you want. If your altar tile has a pentagram, see to it that it points upward, not downward.

Jewelry and Accessories

The use of jewelry and accessories is open to many different interpretations. Wiccans are not really required to wear jewelry during a ritual. However, if you wish to wear any celestial symbol or an amulet, you can wear it. You may also wear a bracelet or a ring that features a special gem or stone.

Crystals and Stones

Crystals and Stones are symbols of the natural element Earth. When used in spells and rituals, they represent the North. They are usually used in healing spells. Sometimes, they are used as foundations for pagan altars.

Crystals are living beings which radiate vibration and are capable of lifting your own vibration simply by being within close proximity to your body. Crystals can be combined with a number of self-help and healing practices for better results.

Some areas where they are finding more usage are meditation, Feng Shui, prayer beads, home or office decoration, energy healing, amulets, baths, fertility and birth, sleep, jewelry, and massage therapy among others.

Through all these uses of crystals, their link to health benefits is helpful to humans as well as animals such as your pets and plants too.

Crystals are as valuable as they are numerous. The wide variety of crystals available today makes it possible for a lover of crystals to choose from a range of options.

The good thing about crystals is that you can enjoy their health benefits regardless of how you use them. Whether you soak them in your bath water, soak them in the water you drink, wear them as ornaments or amulets, place them in a strategic corner of your room or office, put them under your pillow, or hold them while you meditate, you will always get the same health benefits that crystals are known for when you use them correctly.

Normally, each kind of crystal will radiate a particular type of energy that corresponds to and works with the specific energies in certain emotional and physical areas of yourself. Using crystals for healing is as simple as being around them. Other techniques may include holding a crystal in your hand or placing it on a nightstand.

Since these healing crystals are constantly absorbing negative energy in order to provide healing, they can become blocked. Blockages will then reduce the healing effects of the crystals, hence the importance to cleanse them.

Herbs

Another natural tool that symbolizes the North is *Herbs*. Even though they come from the earth, when used for spells, each herb may represent a different natural element.

Various Household Items

At certain points and during certain spells, you may need to use items which are usually found around the home. This could be anything from a potted plant, to sea salt, to a piece of string or even just a glass of water. In these instances, it can be possible to use standard, non-magical items.

Even those items which are just laying around the home will have their own personal and private energies and these can be turned towards better use through the practice of Wicca. As a practical and natural magic, Wicca has a long history of incorporating the everyday and turning it into the magical. As such, do not be surprised to see even the most mundane object become magical when used correctly.

The Book of Shadows

Keep your Book of Shadows on your altar if possible, or very close by if the altar serves more than one function in your house. You will need it for your rituals and spells and for making notes in it during and after a ritual or a spell.

The most important rule to follow when setting up your altar is to do what feels right to you. It is your altar and only you will use it. If something on the altar does not feel right to you or does not carry the particular energy you want, whether it is stimulating or peaceful, then get rid of that item. If you do not find the item to be meaningful then the Divine will not find it meaningful either. If the altar pleases you then it will please the gods and goddesses.

And remember the tools of the altar are symbolic of the meaning that we give to the ceremonies and the spell castings. The seat of your Power is your heart and you must listen to what it says. If you find a better tool and your Heart says it is so, then use that one. And never use any tool that has negativity tied to it. You might have a beautiful ornate mug in your cabinet that could be used as a chalice, but if the person who gave it to you bring up negative memories or feelings it is a good idea to just get rid of the item.

If you associate knives with negative feelings or thoughts then use a beautiful letter opener or similar object for your athame.

The goddesses and gods will speak to us in a language we can understand, and each visit from the Divine is particular to the person themselves. And once you have used your tools a few times then you will know those that speak to you with positive energy and those that need to go. What makes your Heart happy is what is right for you.

Consecrating Magic Tools

The first thing you need to know to use any item is to consecrate it. Consecrating an item is a prerequisite for using it in your spells. If the item is not prepared correctly, then the item will not bond properly with your magical energy, and it may become a drain to the spell instead of its intended purpose.

Therefore, it is very important to take the time to consecrate your magical tools. When you consecrate your items, you bond with them, and they align themselves to your magical energy. Because of the connection between you and your tools, your magic will become more powerful when you use them. Also, note that you may not need each item in this book. You should try to find which ones speak to you.

Follow the steps below to consecrate your items:

1. Create a magic circle with white chalk or table salt.
2. Draw or place a physical pentacle in the middle of the circle.
3. Put each of the tools on the pentacle, usually in the middle of the pentacle.
4. Put a drop of water and salt on the item.
5. Allow a cloud of incense to pass over the item.
6. Say the following invocation:

Oh, Inana! Oh, Dumuzi!

Bless this tool with your divine hands!

Bless this tool with your honor and glory!

How To Prepare Spell Jars

After learning the fundamentals of spells and rituals, you might eventually want to try your hand at crafting your own. This will strengthen your manifestation skills, foster your connection to witchcraft, and deepen your connection to the spiritual world and energies that surround you. Following is a simple breakdown and guidelines on how to get started crafting your own spells and rituals.

1. Set Up an Altar

You do not necessarily need an altar to perform a ritual or cast a spell, but having one is beneficial. Some spellcasters choose not to have altars but don't have a problem with casting their spells. A few spellcasters use their tables or any other surface at home to cast spells. They use a clean, white cloth to cover the surface before they cast the spell. Some choose to sit on the floor instead.

If you look for spells online, you will be asked to sit at an altar before you cast a spell. Why do you think this is important? Before you perform any magic, you need to create a sacred space for yourself to manifest your intent using magic.

2. Preparing the Bath

You need to cleanse yourself of any negative energy before you cast spells, and the best way to remove the energy is to take a ritual bath. This enables you to prepare yourself physically and mentally before you cast the spell or perform rituals. A daily shower does not keep your body fresh and clean, and for this reason, you need to use a ritual bath to calm your body and mind. Not every magic circle will ask you to begin with casting a protection circle, but it is best to draw one around you before you cast spells. This will prevent the entry or movement of bad or negative energy from around you into the circle. You can also prepare yourself mentally through a ritual bath.

3. Defining Your Motives and Intentions

As mentioned earlier, your intentions are very important when it comes to casting spells. You need to know what your intent is and what your end goal is. It is important to be specific when you work with energies. Do not be general because it can add some confusion to the spell. Avoid using negative phrases, sentences, and words in your spell.

You should have good intentions when you cast a spell. Your intent should not affect anybody and should be for your happiness. Having said that, you should understand that spells you cast will affect those around you, so ensure your spell does not harm anybody around you. Only when your thoughts and intentions are pure can your spell work. There can be no negativity in your mind when you cast the spell.

To do this, write your intentions and thoughts down on a piece of paper or in your spiritual journal. This is a great way to frame your desires and use the right words when you cast a spell. As you write it down, you should describe your innermost desire with meaningful and clear words. This will help you understand your wants and needs better. Do not use the phrase 'I want' when you send messages through a spell. It is best to say you are grateful for everything you have.

4. Lighting Candles

Most spells you cast require the use of candles. If you do choose one such spell, you should light it only when you have determined and worded your intent. Place this candle on the altar before you light it. When you do this, it indicates to the universe you are ready to change some aspect of your life. In the realm of magic, a candle is used because it has a connection to the spiritual world.

Different parts of the candle represent different elements in the universe:

- The wax is associated with nature and represents the earth element.
- The hot wax dripping and melting on the side of the candle represents the water element.
- The smoke is associated with the air element.
- Lastly, the flame is associated with purity and represents the fire element.

It is both enlightening and beneficial to use candles when you perform any ritual. Candles not only refresh your mood and change your mindset but also enhance the power of the spell you want to cast. The color of the candle and its flame will attract different types of energies depending on the type of spell you want to cast and your intent. Candles have healing powers and are the main ingredient in any spell you cast, and the color you choose depends on your intent and circumstance.

5. Meditating Before You Cast The Spell

This is an important part of any spell-casting ritual. You should focus on your intent before you begin the spell. The best way to do this is through meditation.

Before you meditate, you need to empty your mind so you can focus only on your intent. This is important if you want your spell to work. According to an experienced spellcaster, meditation is very important if you want to cast spells. You cannot expect the spell to work simply because you use an altar, place all the ingredients on the altar, and pray with candles. The most important aspect is to concentrate on your objective or intent before you cast a spell.

When you perform a spell, you should focus on your goal. This intent and focus will transform into energy. So, don't be doubtful or afraid of what may happen. You also should rid yourself of any negative emotions. The energy you put out into the universe will be scattered and weak before the session ends if you let negativity seep in.

6. Make or Chant a Prayer

Once you focus on your intents, visualize, and meditate, cast the spell. Chant the words you have written down by saying a few words. When you do this, you can send your message to the universe. All you need to do then is to trust the universe will grant your wish. Be very specific about your intent if you want the spell to work for you.

Once you are done with the spell, thank the universe for listening to what you must say.

Symbolic Magical Items and Correspondences Used for Jar Spells

In this section, I will break down some of the more common magical items used and their attached symbolic value or meaning. Correspondences are interchangeable for the most part, and when creating your witch bottle, if an object or ingredient speaks to you, I encourage you to use it.

a. Properties of Herbs and Flowers

Herb	Correspondence
Allspice	Brings luck, attracts money, promotes healing
Anise	Attracts happiness, enhances psychic ability, and wards off curses
Aloe	Family security, protection, and healing
Basil	A wide variety of uses including protection, love, wealth, and banishment of curses. It is also known to dispel weakness and banish fear.
Bay Leaves	Great fortune, healing, strength, improvement of psychic powers, success, banishing negativity, attracting love to you, powerful protection, and attracting your intentions
Black Peppercorns	Protection from negativity and banishment of negativity and evil, increase the power of a spell

Cardamom	Fidelity, lust, and love
Catnip	Love, beauty, happiness, psychic protection when asleep
Celery	Enhancement of psychic and mental powers and ward off evil and negativity
Chamomile	Reduces stresses, promotes calmness, quiet love, and healing
Cayenne Pepper	To increase the power of your spell, and break the bad luck
Chili	Breaking of curses and hexes, attracting love, and promoting fidelity
Cilantro	Prosperity, eloquence, aura cleansing, creativity, and self-expression
Cinnamon	Love, strength, success, spirituality, prosperity, protection, luck, and spirituality
Cloves	Banishing negative and hostile energy, protection, and attracting desires
Clover	Luck, protection, and purification
Coffee	To draw good things to you, and attract positivity
Comfrey	Luck, and healing
Coriander	Aphrodisiac, fertility, protection, a long life, love, lust, and good health
Cumin	For peace and healing
Dandelion	For harmony, freedom, and cleansing of rooms and spaces
Echinacea	Power for charms, herbal mixes, and magical sachets
Eucalyptus	Protection, purifying the home, attracts healing energy
Fennel	Spiritual healing
Flaxseed	Family security, protection of the home, and communication and strength of mind
Frankincense	Success, cleansing, protection, consecration, and safety during meditation
Galangal	Attracting money, breaking curses and hexes, lust, and desire
Garlic	Protection, repulsion of evil spirits, healing, purification, and cleansing
Ginger	Attracting new experiences, sensuality, confidence, prosperity, success, sexuality

Hibiscus	Lust, attracting romance, prophetic dreams, divination
Ivy	To ward off negativity
Jasmine	Clairvoyance, divination, femininity, peace and prosperity
Lavender	Protection, healing, love, cleansing, peace, reducing anxiety, and peaceful resolution
Lemon	Healing, psychic development, spiritual connection, success, and love
Lemongrass	Cleansing of psychic space, opening psychic abilities, lust
Licorice	Lust, love, and fidelity
Mint	Luck, purification, protection in relationships, spirituality, communication, happiness, and attracting good things in your life
Mistletoe	Fertility, ridding misfortune, banishing negative spells, creativity, hung in homes for protection against the elements, and hung in businesses to attract money
Mugwort	For the strength of body and mind
Mustard Seeds	Endurance, courage, to safeguard against injury, strength, and faith
Myrrh	Enhancement of psychic abilities, encourages spiritual awareness
Nettle	Removes fear, enhances courage, hung or sprinkled in homes to dispel evil and negativity
Nutmeg	Clarity, luck and money
Parsley	Wisdom, protection
Red Pepper Flakes	To boost the power of your spell
Rice	To absorb and ward off negativity
Olive Oil	Fertility, lust, potency, peace, healing of the body and mind, and protection
Orange Rind/Peel	Love, femininity, divination, money, blessings, and luck
Passionflower	Prosperity, friendship, lust, libido
Patchouli	Money, love, and luck

Peppermint	Increases energy and vibration, healing, and purification
Pink, Table, or Black Salt	Powerful protection
Rose	Love, peace, fidelity, friendship, and femininity
Rosemary	Love, lust, fidelity, purification, and protection, can substitute or replace any other herb and plant
Sage	Purification of magical objects, self, and home, wisdom, overcoming grief and sharpening mental focus
Sesame Seeds	For happiness, success, and abundance
Sunflower	Wisdom, protection, increases sun energy, attracts wishes
Thyme	Loyalty, love, friendship, wards off grief, courage, banishing negativity and evil, sagely insight, wisdom, and purification
Turmeric	Beauty, used in glamor spells
Vanilla	love, passion, energy, lust, femininity
Yarrow	To calm fears

b. Herbal Substitutes

Sometimes, you will go to cast a spell and realize that you have an ingredient missing, and you just don't have the time, inclination, or money to buy the missing ingredient.

Luckily for you, some herbs and flowers can be substituted for others, and while some recipes may call for specific ingredients, witchcraft is entirely personal to you and what feels right to you. Trust your intuition to make the right substitution choices for your spell.

Herb	Substitute
Angelica	Marigold and calendula
Bergamot	Bee balm flowers, loose leaf Earl Grey tea
Blood	Apple cider vinegar, apple juice
Camphor	Eucalyptus
Carnation	Honeysuckle or Jasmine

Cassia	Cinnamon
Chamomile	White daisies
Citron	Equal parts lemon and orange peel
Citronella	Geranium
Frankincense	Copal or pine resin
Galangal	Ginger
Honey	Maple syrup
Jasmine	Rose
Laurel	Bay leaf
Lemongrass	Lemon balm, freshly grated lemon rind
Mistletoe	Sage or mint
Nettles	Thistle or echinacea
Orange Blossom	Orange peels
Patchouli	Oak moss
Peppermint	Spearmint
Pine Needles	Rosemary
Rose Hip	Rose petals or leaves
Saffron	Orange peels or crocus
Sandalwood	Frankincense
Thyme	Rosemary
Valerian	Catnip
Wine	Grape juice
Wolfsbane	Garlic

c. Gems, Stones, and Crystals

Not all spells call for crystals or gems, and they certainly aren't necessary to perform a spell. Having said that, crystals, gems, and stones are powerful natural materials that are produced by the Earth, and are naturally endowed with certain magical properties. Like herbs, flowers, and plants, some crystals and gems may be more readily available or cheaper than others.

Crystals can be placed directly into your witch bottle or can be stuck into the wax of the jar to increase the magic, absorb negativity, or attract your desires.

Crystals, Stones, or Germs	Correspondence
Agate	Abundance, confidence, courage, creativity, healing, home, love, luck, money, protection, sex, strength, success
Amber	Clarity, creativity, grief, healing, protection, purification, success, wisdom
Amethyst	Creativity, divination, healing, love, peace, prosperity, protection, purification, strength, success, wisdom
Angelite	Anxiety
Aquamarine	Banishing, clarity, creativity, grief, healing, peace, protection, tranquility, travel
Beryl	Clarity, love, romance, travel
Bloodstone	Business, money, success
Blue Lace	Friendship, home
Calcite	Love and romance
Cats Eye	Abundance, luck, prosperity, protection
Celestine	Home
Citrine	Home, luck, protection, success
Desert Rose	Love, romance, peace, spirituality, tranquility

Diamond	Abundance, clarity, confidence, courage, luck, prosperity, protection, wisdom
Dolomite	Grief, negativity
Emerald	Abundance, hexes, love, romance, prosperity, protection, travel
Epidote	Love, romance, protection
Garnet	Confidence, creativity, fertility, fidelity, friendship, home, negativity, strength, success
Jade	Courage, fertility, love, luck, negativity, peace, prosperity, protection, romance, tranquility, travel
Jasper	Abundance, courage, divination, fertility, hexes, love, luck, money, prosperity romance, success
Jet	Divination, hexes
Labradorite	Confidence, courage
Lapis Lazuli	Courage, fidelity, friendship, grief
Lodestone	Confidence
Malachite	Banishing, business
Moonstone	Courage, divination, fertility, friendship, grief, love, romance, strength
Obsidian	Divination, luck, peace, negativity, tranquility
Opal	Abundance, love, luck, prosperity, romance, strength, wisdom
Onyx	Confidence, hexes, negativity
Quartz	Can substitute or replace any other crystal or gem
Pearl	Fertility, love, luck, money, peace, purification, romance, tranquility
Peridot	Abundance, negativity, peace, purity, tranquility
Ruby	Abundance, courage, prosperity, sex
Sapphire	Fertility, fidelity, love, romance, protection

Tiger's eye	Abundance, anxiety, business, confidence, divination, luck, money, negativity, prosperity, strength, success
Topaz	Clarity, courage, fertility, fidelity, home, money, peace, purification, tranquility
Tourmaline	Clarity, courage, creativity, money, negativity, peace, prosperity, sexuality, tranquility
Zircon	Home, sex, sexuality, success

d. Candles

Candles, like herbs, plants, and flowers, are an integral part of witchcraft and magic. You do not need to invest a large amount of money into a candle collection, and regular white or black candles are effective for any spell. If you do choose to buy candles that have a color that corresponds with the spell you're performing, your local home decor shop or supermarket should have the color you are looking for. You do not need to spend much money on building a candle collection. Look out for cheap tea lights or birthday candles at the store. You can even personalize your candles by sticking herbs and flowers to them, or by carving symbols into them.

Candle Color	Correspondence
White	Any spells and can replace any other color candle. Spells for purity, meditation, and healing
Black	Banishing and warding off negative energies, protection, and breaking hexes
Red	Courage, passionate love, passion, libido, lust, and physical attraction
Pink	Romantic love, balance, friendship, relief from depression
Yellow	Mental clarity, manifestation, intellect, knowledge, wisdom
Blue	Creativity, harmony, peace, healing, calm, spirituality
Green	Luck, abundance, grounding, fertility, growth of material goods
Purple	Psychic powers, opportunity, awareness, spiritual development
Orange	Prosperity, success, positivity, emotional healing, ambition

Brown	Stability, security, concentration, animal protection
Light Blue	Peace, serenity, devotions, family harmony, inspiration
Gold	Fortune, fame, power, success, abundance

e. Colors

Colors have a long history of symbolism. Think about royalty and the colors associated with their lineage. Magic is no different, and certain colors come with a set of different associations. Some witches keep a wide range of colored paper, ribbons, strings, inks, and paper to use within their spell work.

Color	Element	Correspondence
Yellow	Air	Communication, subconscious mind, heightening visualization abilities, travel, digestion, nervous system, skin, energy, movement, mental awareness
Orange	Fire	Protection, illumination, personal power, increasing self-worth, luck, energy, positive outcomes
Red	Fire	Protection, strength, willpower, courage, energy, power, blood, birth, lust, sex, war, anger
Pink	Water	Love, acceptance, peace, happiness, joy, laughter, calming, opening, de-stressing
Purple	Earth	Spirituality, mysticism, meditation, psychic work, subconscious mind, healing, peace, removing headaches, mental illness, depression
Blue	Water	Peace, calming emotions, sleep, healing, eliminating inflammations, purification
Green	Water	Healing, fertility, life, plants, gardens, eyes, kidneys, stomach, money, riches, prosperity, luck, love, balance
Black	Earth	Protection, grounding, self-control, resilience, quiet power
White	Water and Earth	Sleep, third eye, protection, removing headache, substitute for any other stone

f. Incense

Incense is used to set a mood and employ your sense of smell when performing a spell. Cones or sticks of incense can be bought from most home goods stores, but some witches will actually make their own incense, blending aromas for their correspondences to add more power to a spell.

Incense	Correspondence
Allspice	Attracting luck, money, increasing physical energy
Bay Leaf	Protection, purification, healing, and increasing psychic powers
Cedar	Protection, purification, healing, spirituality, and attracting money
Cinnamon	Enhance psychic powers, attract money, speed up healing, and confer protection
Clove	Exorcism, love, purification, protection, and increasing money
Dragons Blood	Exorcisms, love, lust, sexual potency, and protection
Fern	Burned indoors to banish evil, and burned outdoors to bring the rain
Frankincense	Banishing evil, spirituality, concentration, and protection
Juniper	Protection, healing, and love
Myrrh	Banishing negativity, peace, consecration, and better meditation
Pine	Healing, warding off evil, and attracting money
Rosemary	Protection, purification, banishing negativity and evil, healing, youthfulness, glamor spells, improving wisdom and intellect
Sage	Healing, spirituality, and cleansing
Sandalwood	Healing, protection, and spirituality
Thyme	Healing, purification, and health

Jar Spell Recipes To Attract Love

1. Attraction Jar

Usage: To attract positive feelings from others
Ingredients:

- A small jar
- Salt
- Pansies
- Pink candle
- Jasmine oil (optional)
- Incense of choice

Procedure:

1. Prepare yourself to cast the spell by meditating for at least 10 minutes.
2. Cleanse the jar with incense.
3. Fill the jar halfway with salt. Fill the other half with dried or fresh pansy petals. If you feel compelled to take this extra step, finish your jar off with a drop of jasmine oil and seal it shut.
4. Melt the pink candle until the wax has formed a seal over the lid or cork of the jar. Keep it on your person or even make it into a necklace to attract the attention of others!

2. Rosy Cheeks Jar

Usage: Attracting romantic love and the admiration of others
Ingredients:

- A small jar
- Salt
- Roses
- Rosewater
- Rose oil
- Red candle
- Incense of choice

Procedure:

1. Prepare yourself to cast the spell by meditating for at least 10 minutes.

2. ○Cleanse the jar with incense.
3. Fill the jar halfway with salt. Add roses, leaving some room at the top.
4. Over the roses add three drops of rose oil and fill the jar the rest of the way with rose water.
5. Place a rose petal over the lid. Melt the red candle until the wax has formed a seal over the lid or cork of the jar, sealing in the petal. Keep this jar on your altar to invite love into your life!

3. Beauty Sleep Jar

Usage: Enhancing your beauty and confidence overnight
Ingredients:

- A medium jar
- Salt
- Violets
- Your favorite perfume
- Rose quartz
- Blue candle
- Incense of choice

Procedure:

1. Prepare yourself to cast the spell by meditating for at least 10 minutes.
2. Cleanse the jar with incense.
3. Fill the jar with salt to your liking, close to three-quarters of the way full if you can. Cover the salt and fill the rest of the jar with violets.
4. Spray your favorite perfume into the jar and then seal it tightly.
5. Melt the blue candle until the wax has formed a seal over the lid or cork of the jar. Charge this jar under the full moon with one rose quartz on top of it. Spray again with perfume if you wish. Keep this jar by your bedside to ensure a restful sleep that is sure to leave you fresh-faced and gorgeous!

4. Pretty in Pink Jar

Usage: Enhancing your natural beauty, presence, and self-confidence
Ingredients:

- A large jar
- Sugar
- Roses
- Pansies

- Rose quartz chips
- Rosewater
- Lilac
- Tulips
- Pink candle
- Incense of choice

Procedure:

1. Prepare yourself to cast the spell by meditating for at least 10 minutes.
2. Cleanse the jar with incense.
3. Fill the jar halfway or two-thirds of the way with sugar. Top the sugar with roses, pansies, lilac, and tulips until the jar is completely full.
4. Use your finger and draw three circles around the rim of the jar with rosewater, whispering your own manifestation for your beauty and confidence while you do it.
5. Seal the jar and sprinkle it with rose quartz chips. Melt the pink candle until the wax has formed a seal over the lid or cork of the jar. Keep this jar in a safe place and your beauty and confidence will only grow!

5. The Soulmate Jar

Usage: For attracting the person you are meant to be with

Ingredients:

- A medium jar
- Salt
- Rose quartz (three)
- Moonstone (three)
- A small piece of paper
- A pen/pencil
- Red candle
- Incense of choice

Procedure:

1. Prepare yourself to cast the spell by meditating for at least 10 minutes.
2. Cleanse the jar with incense.
3. Fill the jar almost all the way with salt, leaving an inch of space or so at the top.
4. Arrange the three moonstones and three rose quartzes in a triangle, each stone touching one of the opposites (One moonstone and one rose quartz, etc.).
5. On the small piece of paper, write this mantra: "My soulmate is mine, they will come to me in time." If you feel compelled, seal this with a kiss or perhaps some rosewater!

6. Place the folded paper in the center of the triangle and seal the jar. Melt the red candle until the wax has formed a seal over the lid or cork of the jar. Move this jar to your altar to manifest your soulmate, but be careful not to jostle the crystal formation within!

6. Oil of Love Jar

Usage: Promoting all-around success in love
Ingredients:

- A medium jar
- Rose oil
- Lavender oil
- Cinnamon oil
- Carrier oil of choice (skin-friendly)
- A small spoon
- Incense of choice

Procedure:

1. Prepare yourself to cast the spell by meditating for at least 10 minutes.
2. Cleanse the jar with incense.
3. Fill the jar with a skin-friendly carrier oil of choice. Add three drops of rose oil, three drops of lavender oil, and three drops of cinnamon oil.
4. Picture your best self. Picture yourself with poise and confidence. Think about this as you stir the mixture clockwise three times with a spoon.
5. Leave this jar on your altar for one full month, then at the end of the month, charge it under the full moon. After that, you can open the jar and use the oil to enhance your beauty magically!

7. Loves Me, Loves Me Not Jar

Usage: Helping you decide what to do, creating romantic clarity
Ingredients:

- A smaller jar
- Sugar
- The whole head of one rose, daisy, or tulip
- Light blue candle
- Incense of choice

Procedure:

1. Prepare yourself to cast the spell by meditating for at least 10 minutes.

2. Cleanse the jar with incense.
3. Fill the jar three-quarters of the way with sugar, leaving enough room inside for movement.
4. Play the game "loves me, loves me not" with the head of the flower you chose, all the while meditating on the answer you seek. Drop all of the petals inside the jar when you have finished plucking them. The answer you seek will be in the "yes" or "no" at the end.
5. When you have received your answer, seal the jar shut with the wax from a light blue candle, but don't get rid of it!
6. In the future, when you are in need of answers or the truth in love, shake the jar. The answer will come to you in time.

8. Dream a Little Dream of Me Jar

Usage: Allowing you to dream of the person you love, and for them to dream of you
Ingredients:

- A medium jar
- Salt
- Blue calcite chips
- Amethyst chips
- Honeysuckle
- Bluebells
- A piece of paper with the name of the one you love written in your handwriting
- Purple candle
- Incense of choice

Procedure:

1. Prepare yourself to cast the spell by meditating for at least 10 minutes.
2. Cleanse the jar with incense.
3. Fill the jar halfway with salt. Place the folded paper with the name of the person you love in the center and cover it with blue calcite and amethyst chips.
4. Fill the rest of the jar with honeysuckle and bluebells and seal it. Melt the purple candle until the wax has formed a seal over the lid or cork of the jar. Keep this jar near your bedside or, if the jar is small enough, keep it under your pillow to dream of your love!

9. Stuck on You Jar

Usage: Binding you and your love together, making yourself irresistible to your romantic prospects

Ingredients:

- A medium jar
- Honey
- Honeysuckle
- Roses
- Rosewater
- Rose oil
- A photo of the person you love, or the person who you want to stick to you
- Red candle
- Incense of choice

Procedure:

1. Prepare yourself to cast the spell by meditating for at least 10 minutes.
2. Cleanse the jar with incense.
3. Fill your jar almost all the way with honey. As you watch it drizzle in, say the mantra: "(Their name) is stuck to me. I am stuck to them." Repeat this as many times as you need to.
4. Once the honey is settled, add three drops of rose oil, rose petals, and honeysuckle. Stir the concoction clockwise three times.
5. Fold up the photo of your loved one and submerge it in the honey. Wet your pointer finger with rose water and draw a circle three more times around the rim of the jar before you seal it.
6. Melt the red candle until the wax has formed a seal over the lid or cork of the jar. Keep this jar on your altar, and turn it over every now and again when you're thinking of your love. They'll be stuck to you in no time!

10. To Attract A Particular Person

Usage: Attracting a specific person to oneself

Warning: this spell may fall under Black Magic, as you are forcing the will of another individual. Make sure that the person you want to attract has feelings toward you. Otherwise, the attraction you would cause in the other person would only be fictitious.

Ingredients:

- A medium-sized dark glass bottle with a cork;
- Rose essential oil;

- Garlic clove;
- Photo of a loved one;
- A picture of you;
- Pen and paper;
- Raw ruby chips;
- A handful of cilantro;
- Red candle for sealing.

Procedure:

1. Begin the ritual with ten minutes of meditation. Think intensely about the person you have chosen, the feelings you get from having that person near you, and imagine how you would feel if you were already a couple;
2. Insert raw ruby chips into the bottle, thinking or saying aloud, "These stones symbolize the fragments of your heart that belong to me, now and forever."
3. Insert the garlic clove into the bottle.
4. Take a piece of paper and write your and your partner's names, then circle them both closed. Finally pour a drop of rose essential oil on it.
5. Roll the paper up like a small parchment and insert it into the bottle.
6. Enter your partner's photo, then your own.
7. Insert a few pinches of cilantro into the bottle.
8. Cork the bottle and place it on a protected surface (a saucer, a box, anything you don't mind ruining).
9. Light the red candle and wait for the wax to melt a little. In the meantime, you can close your eyes again and think intensely about your partner. To make the candle's effect even more powerful, you can preemptively go ahead and do a dressing by steeping it in rose essential oil and then rolling it in a mixture of cinnamon, rose petals and chamomile.
10. Being careful not to burn yourself, pour melted wax over the cap to seal your witch bottle.
11. Now your bottle is ready. Remember that Tuesday is auspicious for love and passion spells, so, if possible, prefer Tuesday to other days to consecrate your love bottle.
12. Hide the bottle away from the view of others and, most importantly, in a place where it will not be touched or moved by anyone.

11.   To Bring An Ex Back

Usage: Attracting an ex to himself

Warning: this spell may fall under Black Magic, as you are forcing the will of another individual. Make sure that the person you want to bring back still has positive feelings for you. Otherwise, the attraction you would cause in the other person would only be fictitious and could be counterproductive.

Ingredients:

- A medium-sized dark glass bottle with a cork;
- Orange blossom;
- Devil's claw;
- A handful of dried coriander;
- Photos of you and your ex(es) together (if you don't have one you can make a collage of two photos or insert a photo of you and a photo of your partner separately);
- Pen and paper;
- Rough rose quartz chips;
- Red candle for sealing.

Procedure:

1. Begin the ritual with ten minutes of meditation. Think intensely about your ex, the feelings of having that person near you, and imagine how you would feel if you were a couple again;
2. Insert orange blossoms into the bottle.
3. Insert the devil's claw into the bottle.
4. Take a piece of paper and write your and your partner's names, then circle them both closed.
5. Roll the paper up like a small parchment and insert it into the bottle.
6. Enter your photo (if you don't have one, enter your ex's first and then your own).
7. Insert a few pinches of dried coriander into the bottle;
8. Insert raw rose quartz chips into the bottle, thinking or saying aloud, "These stones symbolize the fragments of your heart that belong to me, now and forever. By inserting them into this bottle I command you to return to me."
9. Cork the bottle and place it on a protected surface (a saucer, a box, anything you don't mind ruining).
10. Light the pink candle and wait for the wax to melt a little. In the meantime, you can close your eyes and think hard about the rapprochement between you and your ex. To make the candle's effect even more powerful, you can preemptively go ahead and do a dressing by steeping it in rose essential oil and then rolling it in a mixture of cinnamon, rose petals and coriander.

11. Being careful not to burn yourself, pour melted wax over the cap to seal your witch bottle.

12. Now your bottle is ready. Remember that Tuesday is auspicious for love and passion spells, so, if possible, prefer Tuesday to other days to consecrate your love bottle.

13. Hide the bottle away from the view of others and, most importantly, in a place where it will not be touched or moved by anyone.

12.   To Strengthen An Extinguished Love

Usage: Strengthening a pre-existing love
Ingredients:

- A medium-sized dark glass bottle with a cork;
- Orange ribbon or thread;
- Couple photos;
- Chamomile flowers;
- Dehydrated orange peels;
- Lavender sprig;
- A sprig of rosemary;
- Organic honey;
- Pink candle for sealing.

Procedure:

1. Begin the ritual with ten minutes of meditation. Think intensely about your partner, the feelings of having him or her near you, and imagine how you would feel if you were a happy, close-knit couple again;

2. Insert the orange peels into the bottle.

3. Insert your photo taken at a very happy moment into the bottle.

4. Insert the rosemary sprig and the lavender sprig into the bottle.

5. Insert the orange ribbon into the bottle.

6. Cover all the ingredients with organic honey. As you do this think or recite aloud the words, "Let this honey be the glue that brings us together never to be lost again."

7. Cork the bottle and place it on a protected surface (a saucer, a box, anything you don't mind ruining).

8. Light the pink candle and wait for the wax to melt a little. In the meantime, you can close your eyes and think hard about the rapprochement between you and your partner. Being careful not to burn yourself pour the melted wax over the cap to seal your witch bottle.

9. Now your bottle is ready. Remember that Tuesday is auspicious for love and passion spells, so, if possible, prefer Tuesday to other days to consecrate your love bottle.

10. Hide the bottle away from the view of others and, most importantly, in a place where it will not be touched or moved by anyone.

13. To Attract Passionate Love

Usage: Attracting passionate love
Ingredients:

- A medium-sized dark glass bottle with a cork;
- Sugar;
- A handful of dried coriander;
- Cinnamon sticks;
- Dried red rose petals;
- Paper sheet;
- Pen;
- Red candle for sealing

Procedure:

1. Begin the ritual with ten minutes of meditation. Think intensely about your ideal partner, the sensations it causes you, and imagine how you would feel if you were already in the company of your dream partner.
2. Insert three dried red rose petals into the bottle, careful not to break them.
3. Insert a few pinches of dried coriander into the bottle;
4. Insert three cinnamon sticks, one at a time.
5. Take a piece of paper and write down in one sentence what is most important to you in a passionate relationship.
6. Roll the paper up like a small parchment and insert it into the bottle.
7. Pour a few pinches of sugar into the bottle.
8. Cork the bottle and place it on a protected surface (a saucer, a box, anything you don't mind ruining).
9. Light the red candle and wait for the wax to melt a little. In the meantime, you can close your eyes again and think hard about your intentions.
10. Being careful not to burn yourself, pour melted wax over the cap to seal your witch bottle.
11. Now your bottle is ready. Remember that Tuesday is auspicious for love and passion spells, so, if possible, prefer Tuesday to other days to consecrate your love bottle.
12. Hide the bottle away from the view of others and, most importantly, in a place where it will not be touched or moved by anyone.

14. To Attract Eternal Love

Usage: Attracting passionate love

Ingredients:

- A medium-sized dark glass bottle with a cork;
- Organic honey;
- Dried white and rose petals;
- Paper sheet;
- Pen;
- Rose quartz (rough is best);
- Pink Himalayan salt;
- Pink candle for sealing

Procedure:

1. Begin the ritual with ten minutes of meditation. Think intensely about your ideal partner, the sensations it causes you, and imagine how you would feel if you were already in the company of your dream partner.
2. Place three dried white (or rose) rose petals in the bottle, careful not to break them.
3. Insert a few pinches of pink Himalayan salt into the bottle.
4. Place rose quartz in the bottle (rough is best, but you can also use a tumbled stone as long as it has been purified beforehand).
5. Take a piece of paper and write in one sentence the most important aspect of a lasting relationship with you.
6. Roll the leaflet up like a small parchment, dip it generously in organic honey, and then insert it into the bottle.
7. Cork the bottle and place it on a protected surface (a saucer, a box, anything you don't mind ruining).
8. Light the pink candle and wait for the wax to melt a little. In the meantime, you can close your eyes again and think hard about your intentions.
9. Being careful not to burn yourself, pour melted wax over the cap to seal your witch bottle.
10. Now your bottle is ready. Remember that Tuesday is auspicious for love and passion spells, so, if possible, prefer Tuesday to other days to consecrate your love bottle.
11. Hide the bottle away from the view of others and, most importantly, in a place where it will not be touched or moved by anyone.

15. To Seduce Someone

Usage: Seducing someone

Ingredients:

- A medium-sized dark glass bottle with a cork;
- Garlic;
- A handful of dried coriander;
- A sprig of heather;
- Red ribbon;
- Red wine;
- Red rose petals;
- Red candle for sealing.

Procedure:

1. Insert three cloves of garlic into the bottle.
2. Insert a handful of dried cilantro into the bottle.
3. Insert the rosemary sprig and the lavender sprig into the bottle.
4. Insert the red ribbon into the bottle.
5. Insert the red rose petals into the bottle, ensuring they do not break during the procedure.
6. Insert heather sprig.
7. Pour red wine until the bottle is half full.
8. Cork the bottle and place it on a protected surface (a saucer, a box, anything you don't mind ruining).
9. Light the red candle and wait for the wax to melt a little.
10. Being careful not to burn yourself, pour melted wax over the cap to seal your witch bottle.
11. Now your bottle is ready. Remember that Tuesday is auspicious for love and passion spells, so, if possible, prefer Tuesday to other days to consecrate your love bottle.
12. Hide the bottle away from the view of others and, most importantly, in a place where it will not be touched or moved by anyone.

16. To Attract Eternal Love

Usage: Attracting eternal love

Ingredients:

- A medium-sized dark glass bottle with a cork;
- Red ribbon;
- Orchid not yet cut;
- Petals of beauty at night;
- Red or pink glitter;
- Snowflake;
- A natural pearl;
- Three drops of seawater;
- Pink rose petals;
- Absinthe;
- Pink candle for sealing.

Procedure:

1. Insert petals of night beauty into the bottle.
2. Insert the natural pearl into the bottle.
3. Insert the red ribbon into the bottle.
4. Insert the pink rose petals into the bottle, ensuring they do not break off during the procedure.
5. Insert glitter, neither too much nor too little.
6. Recut an orchid flower, the most beautiful on the plant, with disinfected scissors and insert it into the bottle.
7. Pour in absinthe until the bottle is filled.
8. Pour in the three drops of seawater.
9. Have a snowflake fall naturally inside (do not pick it up).
10. Close the bottle with the cork, shake it so the glitter spreads into the liquid, and place it on a protected surface (a saucer, a box, or anything you don't mind ruining).
11. Light the pink candle and wait for the wax to melt a little.
12. Being careful not to burn yourself, pour melted wax over the cap to seal your witch bottle.
13. Now your bottle is ready. Remember that Tuesday is auspicious for love and passion spells, so, if possible, prefer Tuesday to other days to consecrate your love bottle.
14. Hide the bottle away from the view of others and, most importantly, in a place where it will not be touched or moved by anyone.
15. When you find your soul mate get rid of the witch's bottle in a freshwater stream.

17.   To Increase Fertility

Usage: to increase fertility and propitiate pregnancy

Ingredients:

- A medium-sized dark glass bottle with a cork;
- Carnelian;
- Hawthorn berries;
- Wood fern;
- Mandrake root;
- Peach blossom;
- Rose water;
- Pink candle for sealing.

Procedure:

1. Insert hawthorn berries into the bottle.
2. Insert the carnelian into the bottle.
3. Insert mandrake root and wood fern into the bottle.
4. Pour two drops of rosewater on the peach blossom, then place the latter in the bottle.
5. Cork the bottle and place it on a protected surface (a saucer, a box, anything you don't mind ruining).
6. Light the pink candle and wait for the wax to melt a little.
7. Being careful not to burn yourself, pour melted wax over the cap to seal your witch bottle.
8. Now your bottle is ready. Keep in mind that Tuesday is auspicious for love and passion spells, so, if possible, prefer Tuesday to other days to consecrate your love bottle.
9. Hide the bottle in the bedroom, preferably under the mattress.

18. To Avert Betrayal

Usage: Avoiding amorous betrayals

Ingredients:

- A medium-sized dark glass bottle with a cork;
- Licorice;
- Nutmeg;
- Yellow rose petals;
- Wolfsbane leaves;
- Blueberry leaves;
- Pen and paper;
- Red candle for sealing

Procedure:

1. Collect aconite leaves, yellow rose petals and blueberry leaves in a fireproof container. Burn the herbs and collect the ashes.
2. Once the ashes have cooled, pour them into the bottle.
3. Insert three licorice sticks into the bottle.
4. Write your name and your loved one's name on a sheet of paper, then draw a circle around the two names. Insert the folded paper into the bottle.
5. Sprinkle some nutmeg powder into the bottle.
6. Cork the bottle by placing it on a protected surface (a saucer, a box, or anything you don't mind ruining).
7. Light the pink candle and wait for the wax to melt a little.
8. Being careful not to burn yourself, pour melted wax over the cap to seal your witch bottle.
9. Now your bottle is ready. Keep in mind that Tuesday is auspicious for love and passion spells, so, if possible, prefer Tuesday to other days to consecrate your love bottle.
10. Hide the bottle under your loved one's mattress (or side of the bed).

19. For Loving Yourself

Usage: loving oneself

Ingredients:

- A medium-sized dark glass bottle with a cork;
- Pink salt;
- Pink rose petals;
- Rose quartz;
- Dragon's blood (resin);
- Rose water;
- Pink candle for sealing

Procedure:

1. Fill the bottle halfway with pink salt.
2. Insert rose quartz;
3. Add rose petals;
4. Add a teaspoon of dragon's blood;
5. Fill the bottle with rosewater;
6. Cork the bottle by placing it on a protected surface (a saucer, a box, or anything you don't mind ruining).
7. Light the pink candle and wait for the wax to melt a little.
8. Being careful not to burn yourself, pour melted wax over the cap to seal your witch bottle.
9. Now your bottle is ready. Keep in mind that Tuesday is auspicious for love and passion spells, so, if possible, prefer Tuesday to other days to consecrate your love bottle.
10. Keep the bottle with you at all times.

20.   To Foster Couple Communication

Usage: to propitiate couple communication and mutual understanding
Ingredients:

- A small, dark glass bottle with a cork;
- Sodalite chips;
- Rose petals;
- Cornflower;
- Full moon water;
- Pink candle for sealing

Procedure:

1. Fill the bottle halfway with the sodalite chips.
2. Fill the remaining half of the bottle with rose petals and cornflower;
3. Add a few drops of full moon water (the worse your current level of communication, the more drops you insert).
4. Cork the bottle by placing it on a protected surface (a saucer, a box, or anything you don't mind ruining).
5. Light the pink candle and wait for the wax to melt a little.
6. Being careful not to burn yourself, pour melted wax over the cap to seal your witch bottle.
7. Now your bottle is ready. Keep in mind that Tuesday is auspicious for love and passion spells, so, if possible, prefer Tuesday to other days to consecrate your love bottle.
8. Keep the bottle with you at all times.

21.   To Promote Marriage

Usage: Propitiating marriage
Ingredients:

- A medium-sized dark glass bottle with a cork;
- Vase;
- Land of a place you keep happy memories of with your partner;
- Plant with white flowers of your choice;
- Pen
- Couple photos;
- Pink candle for sealing

Procedure:

1. Recruit from the plant all the flowers that have already bloomed and also the buds.
2. Repot the plant in the loaded soil.
3. Put the plant in the room where you spend the most time as a couple (ex: bedroom).
4. When the first flower has bloomed, sever it.
5. Take the bottle and fill it with half-loaded soil.
6. Insert the flower into the bottle.
7. On the back of the photograph write your intention. For example, "When the next flower blooms, our union in marriage will come true."
8. Roll up the photograph and insert it into the bottle.
9. Cover it with the loaded soil.
10. Cork the bottle by placing it on a protected surface (a saucer, a box, or anything you don't mind ruining).
11. Light the pink candle and wait for the wax to melt a little.
12. Being careful not to burn yourself, pour melted wax over the cap to seal your witch bottle.
13. Now your bottle is ready. Keep in mind that Tuesday is auspicious for love and passion spells, so, if possible, prefer Tuesday to other days to consecrate your love bottle.
14. Keep the bottle hidden under your bed or in a safe place.

22. To Make You Say "I Love You"

Usage: to propitiate outpourings of love.
Ingredients:
- A medium-sized dark glass bottle with a cork;
- Sea salt;
- Rose quartz chips;
- Three moonstones;
- Pen and paper;
- Red candle for sealing

Procedure:
1. Fill the bottle halfway with sea salt.
2. Insert rose quartz chips;
3. Insert the three moonstones, one at a time.
4. On the slip of paper write, "I love you, (your name)!" As you do this, imagine your partner's voice as he or she says it to you.
5. Fill the bottle with sea salt to cover all the ingredients.

6. Cork the bottle by placing it on a protected surface (a saucer, a box, or anything you don't mind ruining).

7. Light the red candle and wait for the wax to melt a little.

8. Being careful not to burn yourself, pour melted wax over the cap to seal your witch bottle.

9. Now your bottle is ready. Keep in mind that Tuesday is auspicious for love and passion spells, so, if possible, prefer Tuesday to other days to consecrate your love bottle.

10. Keep the bottle with you at all times.

23. To Strengthen Your Feelings

Usage: Strengthen your feelings toward the other person.

Ingredients:

- A medium-sized dark glass bottle with a cork;
- Lemon and orange peel;
- Rosemary;
- Couple photos;
- Chili pepper;
- Lavender essential oil;
- Rose thorns;
- Red candle for sealing

Procedure:

1. Insert orange and lemon peels into the bottle.

2. Insert your photo taken at a very happy moment into the bottle.

3. Insert the rosemary sprig and dried chili pepper into the bottle.

4. Insert three rose thorns.

5. Add three drops of lavender essential oil.

6. Cork the bottle and place it on a protected surface (a saucer, a box, anything you don't mind ruining).

7. Light the pink candle and wait for the wax to melt a little. In the meantime, you can close your eyes again and think hard about the rapprochement between you and your partner. Being careful not to burn yourself pour the melted wax over the cap to seal your witch bottle.

8. Now your bottle is ready. Keep in mind that Tuesday is auspicious for love and passion spells, so, if possible, prefer Tuesday to other days to consecrate your love bottle.

9. Hide the bottle away from the view of others and, most importantly, in a place where it will not be touched or moved by anyone.

24.   For Magnetic Appeal

Usage: having a magnetic appeal

Ingredients:

- A medium-sized dark glass bottle with a cork;
- Honey;
- Strawberry leaves;
- Red rose petals;
- Rose water;
- Selenite;
- Red candle for sealing

Procedure:

1. Fill the bottle halfway with honey.
2. Insert rose petals and strawberry leaves. As you do so repeat, "As these leaves and petals stick to honey, the fascinated gaze of others sticks to me. So I want and so it shall be."
3. Add a few drops of roses.
4. Add selenite.
5. Cork the bottle by placing it on a protected surface (a saucer, a box, or anything you don't mind ruining).
6. Light the red candle and wait for the wax to melt a little.
7. Being careful not to burn yourself, pour melted wax over the cap to seal your witch bottle.
8. Now your bottle is ready. Keep in mind that Tuesday is auspicious for love and passion spells, so, if possible, prefer Tuesday to other days to consecrate your love bottle.
9. Keep the bottle with you at all times.

25. To Promote Coexistence

Usage: foster coexistence (or improve it)

Ingredients:

- A medium-sized dark glass bottle with a cork;
- Nettles;
- Oak leaf;
- Coarse salt;
- Selenite;
- Brown candle for sealing

Procedure:

1. Fill the bottle halfway with rock salt.
2. Insert oak leaf.
3. Insert nettles (possibly using gloves).
4. Add selenite.
5. Cork the bottle by placing it on a protected surface (a saucer, a box, or anything you don't mind ruining).
6. Light the brown candle and wait for the wax to melt a little.
7. Being careful not to burn yourself, pour melted wax over the cap to seal your witch bottle.
8. Now your bottle is ready. Keep in mind that Tuesday is auspicious for love and passion spells, so, if possible, prefer Tuesday to other days to consecrate your love bottle.
9. Keep the bottle with you at all times or in the house you would like to live in with your partner.

26. For Clarity In The Sentimental Field

Usage: mental clarity for feelings

Ingredients:

- A medium-sized dark glass bottle with a cork;
- Rosemary sprig;
- Raspberry leaves;
- Sandalwood;
- Wild bergamot essential oil;
- Blue candle for sealing.

Procedure:

1. Insert sandalwood into the bottle.
2. Insert the raspberry leaves and add the rosemary sprig.
3. Pour in five drops of wild bergamot essential oil.
4. Cork the bottle and place it on a protected surface (a saucer, a box, anything you don't mind ruining).
5. Light the blue candle and wait for the wax to melt a little. In the meantime, you can close your eyes again and think hard about the rapprochement between you and your partner. Being careful not to burn yourself pour the melted wax over the cap to seal your witch bottle.
6. Now your bottle is ready. Keep in mind that Tuesday is auspicious for love and passion spells, so, if possible, prefer Tuesday to other days to consecrate your love bottle.
7. Hide the bottle under your pillow until you feel you have achieved the desired clarity.

27.   For A United Family

Usage: Keeping relationships with your family together
Ingredients:

- A medium-sized dark glass bottle with a cork;
- Chrysanthemum petals;
- Jasmine petals;
- Lavender sprig;
- Basil leaves;
- Cinnamon stick;
- Rose quartz chips;
- Rose water;
- Family photos;
- White candle for sealing;

Procedure:

1. Write the name of each family member next to his or her head (including animals) on the photograph.
2. Roll up the photograph, then stick it in the bottle.
3. Enter all flowers and herbs.
4. Add two chips of rose quartz for each family member.
5. Insert the cinnamon stick.
6. Pour a drop of rosewater on each family member.

7. Cork the bottle and place it on a protected surface (a saucer, a box, anything you don't mind ruining).

8. Light the white candle and wait for the wax to melt a little. In the meantime, you can close your eyes again and think hard about the rapprochement between you and your partner. Being careful not to burn yourself pour the melted wax over the cap to seal your witch bottle.

9. Now your bottle is ready. Keep in mind that Tuesday is auspicious for love and passion spells, so, if possible, prefer Tuesday to other days to consecrate your love bottle.

10. Hide the bottle at home, away from the sight of your family members.

28. To Mitigate Jealousy

Usage: Mitigating jealousy

Ingredients:

- A medium-sized dark glass bottle with a cork;
- Chamomile;
- Hyaline quartz;
- Sage;
- Lavender essential oil;
- Sunshine water;
- White candle for sealing.

Procedure:

1. Insert chamomile flowers.
2. Insert sage.
3. Add hyaline quartz.
4. Pour in eight drops of lavender essential oil.
5. Fill the bottle with sun water.
6. Cork the bottle and place it on a protected surface (a saucer, a box, anything you don't mind ruining).
7. Light the white candle and wait for the wax to melt a little. In the meantime, you can close your eyes again and think hard about the rapprochement between you and your partner. Being careful not to burn yourself pour the melted wax over the cap to seal your witch bottle.
8. Now your bottle is ready. Keep in mind that Tuesday is auspicious for love and passion spells, so, if possible, prefer Tuesday to other days to consecrate your love bottle.
9. Hide the bottle at home, away from the view of your partner or guests.

29. To Rekindle Passion

Usage: rekindle the fire of passion after years of relationship

Ingredients:

- A medium-sized dark glass bottle with a cork;
- Licorice stick;
- Vanilla stick;
- Olive leaves;
- Violet;
- Red wine;
- Patchouli essential oil;
- Red candle for sealing.

Procedure:

1. Insert one licorice stick and one vanilla stick into the bottle.
2. Insert the olive leaves.
3. Insert violets.
4. Add a few drops of patchouli essential oil.
5. Pour in the red wine until the bottle is almost full.
6. Cork the bottle by placing it on a protected surface (a saucer, a box, anything you don't mind ruining).
7. Light the red candle and wait for the wax to melt a little.
8. Being careful not to burn yourself, pour melted wax over the cap to seal your witch bottle.
9. Now your bottle is ready. Keep in mind that Tuesday is auspicious for love and passion spells, so, if possible, prefer Tuesday to other days to consecrate your love bottle.
10. Hide the bottle under the mattress.

Jar Spell Recipes For Protection

30. For The Protection Of The Family

Usage: protecting the family

Ingredients:

- A medium-sized dark glass bottle with a cork;
- A photo depicting all family members together;
- Coarse salt;
- Pen or marker;
- Disinfectant;
- White tape;
- Hawthorn berries;
- A sprig of acacia;
- White candle for sealing;

Procedure:

1. Write the name of each family member next to his or her head (including animals) on the photograph.
2. Roll up the photograph, fasten it with a white ribbon, and then stick it in the bottle.
3. Insert the acacia sprig into the bottle;
4. Insert hawthorn berries into the bottle, one at a time.
5. Insert a drop of disinfectant for each family member, visualizing healing each of their wounds.
6. Fill the bottle with rock salt.
7. Cork the bottle and place it on a protected surface (a saucer, a box, anything you don't mind ruining).
8. Light the white candle and wait for the wax to melt a little.
9. Being careful not to burn yourself, pour melted wax over the cap to seal your witch bottle.
10. Now your bottle is ready. Keep in mind that Saturday is auspicious for the consecration of protection spells, so, if possible, prefer Saturday to other days to consecrate your protection bottle.
11. Hide the bottle near the entrance gate of your property. If you live in an apartment, find a place near the front door, but be careful that it is not visible or reachable by anyone, especially pets and children.

31.   To Protect The House From Spirits

Usage: to protect the house from evil spirits and the presences

Ingredients:

- Four small dark glass bottles with corks;
- A handful of dried St. John's Wort;
- A handful of dried dill;
- A handful of dried verbena;
- Lavender essential oil;
- Dried rose petals;
- 12 pins;
- White candle for sealing;

Procedure:

1. Carry out candle dressing first by massaging the candle with lavender essential oil from the center upward (drive out, away) and then rolling it in dried rose petals;
2. Insert dried St. John's Wort into the bottles;
3. Insert the dried dill into the bottles;
4. Insert dried verbena into the bottles;
5. Insert three pins for each bottle, one at a time, and drop them pointwise (as if you were trying to stab something).
6. Place one drop of lavender essential oil in each small bottle;
7. Cork the bottles and place them on a protected surface (a saucer, a box, anything you don't mind ruining).
8. Light the white candle and wait for the wax to melt a little.
9. Being careful not to burn yourself, pour melted wax over the cap to seal your witch bottles.
10. Now your protection bottles are ready. Keep in mind that Saturday is auspicious for the consecration of protection spells, so, if possible, prefer Saturday to other days to consecrate your protection bottles.
11. Hide the bottles in the four corners of the house, in a hidden place unreachable by others.

32. For Protection From The Envy Of Others

Usage: protecting oneself from others' envy

Ingredients:

- A small, dark glass bottle with a cork;
- A picture of you;
- Coarse salt;
- White silk ribbon;
- Pen;
- Paper sheet;
- White candle for sealing;

Procedure:

1. Roll up your photo and close it with the white silk ribbon;
2. Insert the photo into the bottle;
3. Insert three grains of coarse salt into the bottle;
4. On a card write the following formula: "Let any wrong or evil addressed to me be shielded by this bottle."
5. Roll up the card like a scroll and insert it into the bottle;
6. Cork the bottle and place it on a protected surface (a saucer, a box, or anything you don't mind ruining).
7. Light the white candle and wait for the wax to melt a little.
8. Being careful not to burn yourself, pour melted wax over the cap to seal your witch bottle.
9. Now your bottle is ready. Keep in mind that Saturday is auspicious for the consecration of protection spells, so, if possible, prefer Saturday to other days to consecrate your protection bottle.
10. Carry your bottle with you, in a pocket or purse. You mustn't let anyone touch your protection bottle. The power of this protection bottle runs out every three months, so to stay protected create another one. You can only recycle your photo from the old bottle, all other ingredients must be replaced and the old contents burned.

33.   For Personal Protection

Usage: personal protection and that of our loved ones

Ingredients:

- A small amber glass bottle with cork;
- A handful of dried mugwort;
- A handful of dried juniper;
- A handful of dried rosemary;
- A handful of dried thyme;
- Pine needles;
- 3 strands of black wool 3 cm long;
- 3 nails;
- 3 rose or cactus thorns (optional);
- Moon eclipse water or red wine;
- A hair of the person to be protected;
- Black or red candle for sealing.

Procedure:

1. Insert the hair of the person to be protected into the small bottle. Make sure it got into it and didn't stick to your fingers or the mouth of the bottle - it can happen.
2. Close your eyes and focus for a few seconds on the person for whom the bottle of protection is intended.
3. Insert the needles one at a time, taking care to drop them on the tip, as if you were trying to pierce something.
4. Repeat the process for rose and cactus thorns, being careful to tip them.
5. Now drown the negativity by pouring eclipse moon water or red wine. Caution: if you use powerful liquids such as lunar eclipse water be sure to use only a few drops, otherwise the spell may backfire.
6. Insert the three strands of black wool, one at a time.
7. Mix the five dried herbs (rosemary, thyme, pine needles, juniper, and mugwort), then place the mix in the bottle until it is full or the mixture is finished.
8. Cork the bottle and place it on a protected surface (a saucer, a box, anything you don't mind ruining).
9. Light the candle (possibly black) and wait for the wax to melt.
10. Being careful not to burn yourself, pour melted wax over the cap to seal your witch bottle.

11. Now your bottle is ready. Keep in mind that Saturday is auspicious for the consecration of protection spells, so, if possible, choose Saturday to other days to consecrate your protection bottle.

34. For House Protection

Usage: Protection of one's dwelling

Ingredients:

- A medium-sized amber glass bottle with cork;
- A handful of dried rosemary;
- 3 needles;
- 3 pins;
- Red wine;
- A black candle for sealing.

Procedure:

1. Insert the three needles into the bottle, one at a time, taking care to drop them on the tip as if you were trying to pierce something.
2. Insert the three pins into the bottle, one at a time, again being careful to drop them pointwise.
3. Cover the needles and pins with dried rosemary.
4. Fill with red wine to drown out negativity and bad influences.
5. Cork the bottle and place it on a protected surface (a saucer, a box, or anything you don't mind ruining).
6. Light the candle (black or red) and wait for the wax to melt.
7. Being careful not to burn yourself, pour melted wax over the cap to seal your witch bottle.
8. Now your bottle is ready. Keep in mind that Saturday is auspicious for the consecration of protection spells, so, if possible, prefer Saturday to other days to consecrate your protection bottle.
9. Bury the protection bottle in the farthest corner of your property to allow the spell to keep negative influences as far away from you and your home as possible.
10. If you bury it in the ground, you can draw a pentagram in the earth above the bottle to increase the power of the protection spell.
11. If you live in an apartment, you can opt to hide the protective bottle in the house, but be careful to prepare a place not visible or accessible to others.

35. For The Protection Of Spaces

Usage: Protect your own space outside your home (e.g., the office where you work)

Ingredients:

- A medium-sized dark glass bottle with a cork;
- 7 nails, preferably old and rusty;
- 1 teaspoon dried rosemary;
- A handful of black salt;
- A black candle for sealing.

Procedure:

1. Insert the seven needles into the bottle, one at a time, taking care to drop them on the tip as if you were trying to pierce something.
2. Cover the needles with dried rosemary.
3. Cover with black salt.
4. Cork the bottle and place it on a protected surface (a saucer, a box, anything you don't mind ruining).
5. Light the black candle and wait for the wax to melt a little.
6. Being careful not to burn yourself, pour melted wax over the cap to seal your witch bottle.
7. Now your bottle is ready. Keep in mind that Saturday is auspicious for the consecration of protection spells, so, if possible, prefer Saturday to other days to consecrate your protection bottle.
8. Hide the protection bottle in the room you want to protect, but be careful to put it in a place not visible or accessible to others.

36. For The Protection Of One's Animals

Usage: Pet and non-pet protection

Ingredients:

- A medium-sized dark glass bottle with a cork;
- A hair of the animal;
- A paper card;
- Pen;
- 3 ivy leaves;
- A handful of catnip;
- A handful of dried Rosemary;
- Brown candle (animal propitiation) for sealing.

Procedure:

1. Insert the animal hair into the bottle (be careful that it has fallen to the bottom and not stuck to your fingers or the neck of the bottle-it can happen);
2. Write your pet's name on the slip of paper, then roll the slip of paper up like a tiny parchment and drop it inside the bottle;
3. Insert a pinch of dried rosemary into the bottle;
4. Insert the three ivy leaves into the bottle, one at a time, taking care that they do not break in the process;
5. Insert a handful of catnip into the bottle.
6. Cork the bottle and place it on a protected surface (a saucer, a box, anything you don't mind ruining).
7. Light the brown candle and wait for the wax to melt a little.
8. Being careful not to burn yourself, pour melted wax over the cap to seal your witch bottle.
9. Now your bottle is ready. Keep in mind that Saturday is auspicious for the consecration of protection spells, so, if possible, prefer Saturday to other days to consecrate your protection bottle.
10. Hide the bottle in a place your pet frequents a lot, such as where his or her kennel is, but be careful to hide it out of sight and, most importantly, in a place where it will not be touched or moved by anyone but you;
11. If, on the other hand, you created the protection bottle to protect your farm animals, you can opt to bury the bottle in a corner of the pen, barn, chicken coop or place where you keep your animals safe.

37. For The Protection Of Children And Infants

Usage: protection of children and infants from negative influences

Ingredients:

- A medium-sized dark glass bottle with a cork;
- A handful of hawthorn berries;
- Anise;
- Basil leaves;
- A sprig of acacia;
- Pen;
- Paper sheet;
- White candle for sealing;

Procedure:

1. Write on the slip of paper the name of the child you want to protect, then roll the slip of paper up like a tiny parchment and drop it inside the bottle;
2. Insert a handful of star anise into the bottle;
3. Insert the acacia sprig into the bottle;
4. Insert hawthorn berries into the bottle, one at a time;
5. Insert the basil leaves into the bottle, one at a time, taking care that they do not break in the process;
6. Cork the bottle and place it on a protected surface (a saucer, a box, anything you don't mind ruining).
7. Light the white candle and wait for the wax to melt a little.
8. Being careful not to burn yourself, pour melted wax over the cap to seal your witch bottle.
9. Now your bottle is ready. Keep in mind that Saturday is auspicious for the consecration of protection spells, so, if possible, prefer Saturday to other days to consecrate your protection bottle.
10. Hide the bottle in the child's room for whom you intended the spell, but be very careful to hide it away from the sight of others and, above all, in a place where it will not be touched or moved by anyone but you.

38. For Negative Vibes

Usage: check for negative vibrations within a confined environment
Ingredients:

- A medium-sized container made of clear glass;
- Coarse salt;
- Apple vinegar

Procedure:

1. Place three tablespoons of coarse salt in the clear glass container;
2. Cover the salt with apple cider vinegar until it almost fills the container;
3. Place the container in the room of your choice, preferably in a corner, and make sure no one moves it from there or touches it for the next twenty-four hours.
4. After twenty-four hours have passed, check the state of the salt. If nothing has changed, the chosen environment is not permeated with negative vibrations, so you can simply move the container to another room and repeat the process.
5. If, on the other hand, the salt has risen to the surface, climbing the walls of the container, it has activated its power to absorb negative energies. In this case, flush the mixture down the toilet and rinse the container very well before repeating the process in another room. To clean a room permeated with negative energies you can use palo

santo or white sage, open windows wide to make air exchange and clean floors and surfaces with water and coarse salt.

6. If the salt has taken on a strange color (often greenish) there is likely a curse or the presence of some dark entity. In this case, you will have to proceed with the purification of the room.

39. To Protect Oneself From Misfortune

Usage: to protect oneself from misfortune

Ingredients:

- A medium-sized dark glass bottle with a cork;
- 100 red rose petals;
- Freshly picked moss;
- Oregano;
- Holy water (or disinfectant);
- Mortar and pestle;
- White candle for sealing;

Procedure:

1. Peel off 100 red rose petals and place them in a container of holy water for one hour.
2. After an hour has elapsed, remove the petals from the holy water, put them in a mortar and pound them to make juice.
3. Pour the resulting juice into the bottle.
4. Insert moss into the bottle.
5. Place a handful of oregano in the bottle.
6. Cork the bottle and place it on a protected surface (a saucer, a box, anything you don't mind ruining).
7. Light the white candle and wait for the wax to melt a little.
8. Being careful not to burn yourself, pour melted wax over the cap to seal your witch bottle.
9. Now your bottle is ready. Keep in mind that Saturday is auspicious for the consecration of protection spells, so, if possible, prefer Saturday to other days to consecrate your protection bottle.
10. Hold the bottle under your bed until the color of the mixture changes color. When this happens, it means the bottle has done its job, so undo it.

40. To Protect Against Negative Influences

Usage: Protection from negative influences
Ingredients:

- A medium-sized amber glass bottle with cork;
- A handful of dried rosemary;
- Galbanum sprig;
- Lavender sprig;
- Needles or pins;
- Nettles;
- Olive leaves;
- A white candle for sealing.

Procedure:

1. Insert the dried rosemary into the bottle.
2. Insert the galbanum sprig and the lavender sprig into the bottle.
3. Insert three pins into the bottle, one at a time, and drop them pointwise (as if you were trying to stick something).
4. Insert a handful of nettles (possibly using a glove).
5. Cork the bottle and place it on a protected surface (a saucer, a box, or anything you don't mind ruining).
6. Light the white candle and wait for the wax to melt a little.
7. Being careful not to burn yourself, pour melted wax over the cap to seal your witch bottle.
8. Now your bottle is ready. Keep in mind that Saturday is auspicious for the consecration of protection spells, so, if possible, prefer Saturday to other days to consecrate your protection bottle.
9. Keep the bottle with you always in your pocket or purse.

41. For Generic Protection

Usage: Attracting good fortune in business
Ingredients:

- A medium-sized amber glass bottle with cork;
- Rosemary sprig;
- Coffee grounds;
- Tiger eye chips;
- Parsley;

- Lavender essential oil;
- White candle for sealing.

Procedure:

1. Insert coffee grounds into the bottle.
2. Pour in the fresh parsley.
3. Pour in the tiger eye chips.
4. Add a few drops of lavender essential oil.
5. Insert the rosemary sprig.
6. Cork the bottle and place it on a protected surface (a saucer, a box, anything you don't mind ruining).
7. Light the white candle and wait for the wax to melt a little.
8. Being careful not to burn yourself, pour melted wax over the cap to seal your witch bottle.
9. Now your bottle is ready. Keep in mind that Saturday is auspicious for the consecration of protection spells, so, if possible, prefer Saturday to other days to consecrate your protection bottle.
10. Keep the bottle with you at all times or in the room where you spend most of your time.

42. To Protect One's Memories

Usage: protecting memories and memory

Ingredients:

- A medium-sized amber glass bottle with cork;
- Artemisia;
- Poppy seeds;
- Elderflower;
- Adularia (moonstone);
- Full moon water;
- Silver candle for sealing.

Procedure:

1. Insert the poppy seeds into the bottle, one at a time.
2. Insert adularia into the bottle.
3. Add mugwort and elderflower.
4. Add a few drops of full-moon water.
5. Cork the bottle and place it on a protected surface (a saucer, a box, anything you don't mind ruining).

6. Light the silver candle and wait for the wax to melt a little.

7. Being careful not to burn yourself, pour melted wax over the cap to seal your witch bottle.

8. Now your bottle is ready. Keep in mind that Saturday is auspicious for the consecration of protection spells, so, if possible, prefer Saturday to other days to consecrate your protection bottle.

9. Keep the bottle with you at all times or under your pillow.

43. To Protect Against Accidents

Usage: protecting yourself from accidents

Ingredients:

- A medium-sized amber glass bottle with cork;
- Onion;
- Rosemary sprig;
- Jade chips;
- Black salt;
- Sunshine water;
- Yellow candle for sealing.

Procedure:

1. Cut the onion in half and insert it into the bottle.

2. Pour in the jade chips, one at a time.

3. Add black salt, one grain at a time. As you do this, visualize the salt grains building your invisible armor against accidents.

4. Add a few drops of sun water.

5. Insert the rosemary sprig into the bottle.

6. Cork the bottle and place it on a protected surface (a saucer, a box, or anything you don't mind ruining).

7. Light the yellow candle and wait for the wax to melt a little.

8. Being careful not to burn yourself, pour melted wax over the cap to seal your witch bottle.

9. Now your bottle is ready. Keep in mind that Saturday is auspicious for the consecration of protection spells, so, if possible, prefer Saturday to other days to consecrate your protection bottle.

10. Keep the bottle with you at all times or, if you own a car or other vehicle, keep it under the driver's seat.

44.   To Protect Oneself From The Evil Eye

Usage: to protect oneself from the evil eye
Ingredients:

- A medium-sized amber glass bottle with cork;
- Hyssop sprig;
- Viburnum sprig;
- Amethyst chips;
- Rose thorns;
- Lavender essential oil;
- Purple candle for sealing

Procedure:

1. Insert the sprig of hyssop into the bottle.
2. Insert the viburnum sprig into the bottle.
3. Pour in the amethyst chips, one at a time.
4. Add rose thorns, one at a time. As you do this, visualize that each thorn is protecting you from the evil eye like an armor.
5. Add three drops of lavender essential oil.
6. Cork the bottle and place it on a protected surface (a saucer, a box, or anything you don't mind ruining).
7. Light the yellow candle and wait for the wax to melt a little.
8. Being careful not to burn yourself, pour melted wax over the cap to seal your witch bottle.
9. Now your bottle is ready. Keep in mind that Saturday is auspicious for the consecration of protection spells, so, if possible, prefer Saturday to other days to consecrate your protection bottle.
10. Keep the bottle with you always and don't let anyone touch it.

45.   To Protect Beauty

Usage: to protect one's beauty and youthfulness
Ingredients:

- A small amber glass bottle with a cork;
- Dried rose petals;
- Dried hibiscus flowers;
- Galangal root;
- Sapphire chips;

- Lavender essential oil;
- Purple candle for sealing

Procedure:

1. Place rose petals and dried hibiscus flowers in the bottle.
2. Insert the galangal root into the bottle.
3. Pour in the sapphire chips, one at a time.
4. Add three drops of lavender essential oil.
5. Cork the bottle and place it on a protected surface (a saucer, a box, or anything you don't mind ruining).
6. Light the purple candle and wait for the wax to melt a little.
7. Being careful not to burn yourself, pour melted wax over the cap to seal your witch bottle.
8. Now your bottle is ready. Keep in mind that Saturday is auspicious for the consecration of protection spells, so, if possible, prefer Saturday to other days to consecrate your protection bottle.
9. Keep the bottle with you always and don't let anyone touch it.

46. To Protect Plants

Usage: protecting plants

Ingredients:

- A small amber glass bottle with a cork;
- A handful of fertile soil;
- Cinnamon powder;
- Coffee beans;
- Jade chips;
- Full moon water;
- Green or brown candle for sealing.

Procedure:

1. Insert the coffee beans into the bottle.
2. Insert fertile soil into the bottle.
3. Add jade chips and cinnamon powder.
4. Add a few drops of full-moon water;
5. Cork the bottle and place it on a protected surface (a saucer, a box, or anything you don't mind ruining).
6. Light the green candle and wait for the wax to melt a little.

7. Being careful not to burn yourself, pour melted wax over the cap to seal your witch bottle.

8. Now your bottle is ready. Keep in mind that Saturday is auspicious for the consecration of protection spells, so, if possible, prefer Saturday to other days to consecrate your protection bottle.

9. Bury the bottle in the pot of the plant to be protected. You can also bury it in the garden or vegetable garden, but it is advisable to make more than one by burying them in the corners of the garden.

47. To Protect Oneself From Addiction

Usage: protecting oneself from addiction
Ingredients:

- A small amber glass bottle with a cork;
- Blueberries;
- Ivy leaves;
- Holy thistle;
- Red wine;
- Aloe vera;
- Eucalyptus;
- Purple candle for sealing.

Procedure:

1. Insert the blueberries into the bottle, one at a time.
2. Insert ivy and holy thistle into the bottle.
3. Insert a slice of aloe vera into the bottle.
4. Add eucalyptus.
5. Fill the bottle with red wine.
6. Cork the bottle and place it on a protected surface (a saucer, a box, or anything you don't mind ruining).
7. Light the purple candle and wait for the wax to melt a little.
8. Being careful not to burn yourself, pour melted wax over the cap to seal your witch bottle.
9. Now your bottle is ready. Keep in mind that Saturday is auspicious for the consecration of protection spells, so, if possible, prefer Saturday to other days to consecrate your protection bottle.
10. Keep the bottle with you always and do not let anyone touch it.

48. For Protection From Thieves

Usage: to protect against thieves and theft
Ingredients:

- A medium-sized amber glass bottle with cork;
- Amethyst chips;
- Juniper berries;
- Red wine;
- Rosemary sprig;
- Monetines;
- Padlock;
- A white candle for sealing.

Procedure:

1. Insert rosemary into the bottle.
2. Pour the amethyst chips into the bottle.
3. Insert the padlock into the bottle (it must be locked and keyless).
4. Insert the coins, one at a time.
5. Insert juniper berries;
6. Pour red wine until the bottle is full.
7. Cork the bottle and place it on a protected surface (a saucer, a box, or anything you don't mind ruining).
8. Light the white candle and wait for the wax to melt a little.
9. Being careful not to burn yourself, pour melted wax over the cap to seal your witch bottle.
10. Now your bottle is ready. Keep in mind that Saturday is auspicious for the consecration of protection spells, so, if possible, prefer Saturday to other days to consecrate your protection bottle.
11. Keep the bottle with you always in your pocket or purse.

49. To Protect Oneself From Assailants

Usage: to protect oneself from malicious attackers
Ingredients:

- A medium-sized amber glass bottle with cork;
- A handful of dried mugwort;
- A handful of dried rosemary;
- A handful of euphorbia;

- Amethyst;
- 3 nails;
- Moon eclipse water;
- Black or red candle for sealing.

Procedure:

1. Insert the rosemary and mugwort into the bottle.
2. Insert the amethyst into the bottle.
3. Insert juniper berries and euphorbia.
4. Pour ten drops of eclipse moon water.
5. Insert three rusty nails.
6. Cork the bottle and place it on a protected surface (a saucer, a box, or anything you don't mind ruining).
7. Light the white candle and wait for the wax to melt a little.
8. Being careful not to burn yourself, pour melted wax over the cap to seal your witch bottle.
9. Now your bottle is ready. Keep in mind that Saturday is auspicious for the consecration of protection spells, so, if possible, prefer Saturday to other days to consecrate your protection bottle.
10. Keep the bottle with you always in your pocket or purse.

Jar Spell Recipes To Attract Wealth

50. To Always Have Money

Usage: If you want to have money whenever you need it, to make purchases, invest in new businesses, or enjoy yourself, this spell will help you.

Ingredients:

- Pyrite
- Citrine
- Cinnamon
- Basil
- Dragon blood
- Money oil
- Oregano
- Golden candle
- Oil of abundance
- Jar

Procedure:

1. Light the gold candle and purify the jar.
2. Imagine that you have all the money in the world, more than you need, that you put your hand in your pocket and there is a lot. Visualize that image and start putting all the ingredients in the jar.
3. When finished, seal with gold wax.
4. Have it with you or wherever you want the money to gush.

51. Good Luck All Year

Usage: This is a ritual to have good luck all year long; that you do well in business, at work, and in whatever you set out to do.

Ingredients:

- 7 gold coins
- 7 silver coins
- A handful of wheat
- A handful of rice
- Cloves

- Cinnamon
- Large jar with lid
- Golden candle

Procedure:

1. Light the candle and begin the meditation process. Purify the entire jar inside and out with the flame.
2. As you meditate, place all the ingredients as your intuition indicates.
3. Make the request while you are in the meditation process and you will see how it will come to you.
4. When finished, close it, place gold wax around it, and put the jar close to where you want prosperity to improve.

52. To Attract Fortune

Usage: If you are looking to have a fortune, collect an inheritance, win the lottery, or have financial comfort, this is a good spell.

Ingredients:

- Jar
- Jade and aventurine crystals
- Jade plant
- Ginger
- Thyme
- Seeds you want
- Rice
- Paper and pen
- Yellow candle

Procedure:

1. Light the candle and purify the jar. Begin to meditate while thinking about how you will see yourself with money or whatever you have in mind.
2. Meditating, write on the paper: "Money flows to me."
3. You can add all the ingredients to the jar leaving the folded paper in the middle.
4. Say the intention out loud.
5. Seal the jar with the candle wax and put it where you will see it frequently so you don't forget your intention.

53. To Be Successful in Business

Usage: Whether you are starting a business or want to close an important contract, this spell will help you.

Ingredients:

- Rosemary
- Tiger's Eye
- Sea salt
- Green aventurine
- Smoky quartz
- Yellow candle
- Jar

Procedure:

1. Light the yellow candle as you think about that business, being successful, having franchises, whatever size you want. No matter how big it is, the bigger the better.
2. Meditate with that image and start placing the ingredients in the jar until it is full.
3. In the end, seal with yellow wax.
4. Place this near where you want the business to be, in the space you want to have wealth.
5. You can recharge it on a new moon.

54. Coin Jar

Usage: Attracting material wealth, money, and financial success

Ingredients:

- A medium jar
- Salt
- Basil
- Cinnamon sticks
- Citrine
- Allspice
- Incense of choice

Procedure:

1. Prepare yourself to cast the spell by meditating for at least 10 minutes.
2. Cleanse the jar with incense.

3. Pour salt into the bottom of the jar and sprinkle with basil and allspice. Place the cinnamon sticks and citrine in the center. Then, place five coins in the jar at the points of the pentacle.

4. Leave the jar closed on your altar. Return to the jar whenever money, success, or prosperity comes to you and add more coins or even bills. The more you put into it, the more you can get out of it!

5. Repeat until the jar is filled, or you no longer have use for the spell.

55. Aventurine Jar

Usage: Manifesting future wealth and success
Ingredients:

- A small jar
- Salt
- Aventurine chips
- Green candle
- Incense of choice

Procedure:

1. Prepare yourself to cast the spell by meditating for at least 10 minutes.
2. Cleanse the jar with incense.
3. Fill the jar halfway with salt. Fill the other half of the jar with small aventurine chips. Seal the jar firmly.
4. Melt the green candle until the wax has formed a seal over the lid or cork of the jar. Speak the phrase: "Money is already mine." Repeat this phrase as many times as you need!
5. Place this jar on your altar or carry it on your person to manifest success.

56. Cinnamon Jar

Usage: Securing luck for future endeavors, especially in job searches
Ingredients:

- A medium jar
- Ground cinnamon
- Cinnamon sticks
- Peppermint oil
- Carrier oil of choice
- Green candle
- Incense of choice

Procedure:

1. Prepare yourself to cast the spell by meditating for at least 10 minutes.
2. Cleanse the jar with incense.
3. Place as many cinnamon sticks inside the jar as you want. Sprinkle ground cinnamon liberally around the cinnamon sticks.
4. In a separate bowl, mix your carrier oil of choice with three drops of peppermint oil until they are completely combined.
5. Pour the combined oils over the cinnamon sticks until the jar is completely full, then seal it tightly.
6. Melt the green candle until the wax has formed a seal over the lid or cork of the jar. Leave this jar on your altar to manifest good luck!

57. Poor Men Prosper Jar

Usage: Manifesting a shift from rags to riches, letting go of that which no longer serves you

Ingredients:

- A leftover jar (any size)
- A lighter or matches
- Old pay stubs, rejection letters, termination notices—anything that has led you to struggle, or that you have been having trouble overcoming
- Athame (optional)
- White candle
- Incense of choice

Procedure:

1. Prepare yourself to cast the spell by meditating for at least 10 minutes. For this spell, also make sure that you are away from anything flammable, and that you are taking care when using fire.
2. Cleanse the jar with incense.
3. Take your collected papers in your hands. Look at them. Feel the way their contents affect you, and allow yourself to let go of the negativity they have brought to you. If you don't have printed papers for some of these, feel free to write them out yourself.
4. Cut or tear up these papers into small pieces. You have the option of slicing them with an athame if you have one.
5. Put them into the jar and use your lighter or matches to burn them.
6. Once the flame has completely died down and there is no smoldering left, stop up the jar. Melt the white candle until the wax has formed a seal over the lid or cork of the jar.

7. Keep this jar wherever you need it. On your desk, at your place of work, on your nightstand—wherever it will remind you of your progress!

58. Manifestation Jar

Usage: Manifesting future events or successes
Ingredients:

- A small jar
- Salt
- Bay leaves
- Pyrite chips
- A pen/pencil
- Green candle
- Incense of choice

Procedure:

1. Prepare yourself to cast the spell by meditating for at least 10 minutes.
2. Cleanse the jar with incense.
3. Fill the jar with salt and sprinkle pyrite chips on top, leaving space at the top of the jar.
4. Lay out your bay leaves in front of you. Think about the things that you want to invite into your life. Meditate on those things while writing each of them on their own bay leaf.
5. Crush the leaves one by one and put them in the jar.
6. Melt the green candle until the wax has formed a seal over the lid or cork of the jar. Place this jar on your altar, and keep an eye out for those events and successes in the coming weeks!

59. To Increase Productivity

Usage: If you are working on a project or if you want to improve your work performance, this is a spell that can help you.
Ingredients:

- Cinnamon
- Vanilla
- Citrine
- Sage
- Clove
- Red candle

- Glass jar

Procedure:

1. Light the candle and imagine that you produce everything you want, and that you are unstoppable. Meditate on seeing yourself like this and purify the jar.
2. Begin to place all the ingredients inside, one by one, calmly.
3. When full, seal with red wax.
4. Keep the jar handy at all times so you can increase productivity. When you feel that you have achieved it, discard the spell.

60.   For Good Luck

Usage: If you want to have good luck in business and life in general, apply this spell according to your wishes.

Ingredients:

- Salt
- White rice
- String
- Bay leaves
- Green candle
- Glass jar

Procedure:

1. Light the green candle and imagine that you have all the luck in the world. Imagine that you find a lottery ticket with all the winning numbers, or however you want.
2. Start placing all the ingredients inside, one by one, while imagining that luck touches your life and never goes away.
3. When finished, seal with green wax.
4. Have it on hand at home, wherever you see it. You can decorate it with golden elements that emulate gold.

61.   Spell With the Support of the Moon to Attract Wealth

Usage: The moon has power and you can use it to attract wealth. With this spell that you will do on a new moon, you will be reborn with wealth from now on.

Ingredients:

- Basil
- Bay leaves
- Chamomile
- Whole clove

- Tiger eye crystals
- Patchouli essential oil
- Bee wax
- Incense
- Green candle
- Jar

Procedure:

1. Light the green candle while imagining that you attract money and that good fortune touches your life.
2. Start placing the ingredients when you see that you get what you are looking for.
3. As you place them, you see how prosperity and wealth grow in you.
4. Putting everything in, cover, heat the beeswax, and then roll around the jar decorating however you like.
5. Keep it close so you can see it and always remember it.

62. Get Prosperity

Usage: If prosperity flees you or you want to attract more, this is a spell that can help you.

Ingredients:

- Sea salt
- Cinnamon
- Mint
- Almonds
- Dill
- Acorn
- Pine tree
- Orange
- Jasmine
- Jar
- Golden candle

Procedure:

1. Light the candle and purify the jar.
2. Imagine that you have a lot of prosperity and that everything goes as you wish. Meditate on it while you begin to place the ingredients.
3. Finish placing all the ingredients.
4. Seal with gold wax and decorate with it as you like.

63. To Close a Deal

Usage: If you have a pending business to do or you want it to be done, with this spell you will achieve it.

Ingredients:

- Basil
- Jasmine
- Pachira
- Pilea peperomioides
- Bamboo
- Pyrite
- Green candle
- Jar

Procedure:

1. Light the candle and purify the jar.
2. Meditate focusing on the amount of money you want to bring into your life and how you achieve it while holding the jar.
3. Put it on the altar and start placing the ingredients inside one by one.
4. When finished, seal with green wax.
5. Leave the spell on the altar. You can surround it with salt and put the candle on until it burns out next to it.

64. Prosperity Taking Advantage of the New Moon

Usage: Wait for the new moon so that you get the desired effect in this spell. It will help you attract prosperity into your life at a great speed.

Ingredients:

- Jar
- Basil
- Chamomile
- Bay leaves
- Whole clove
- Oil of abundance
- Yellow candle
- Clear quartz crystal

Procedure:

1. Light the candle and purify the jar. Imagine that you have the prosperity you desire.

2. Start placing all the ingredients inside while still visualizing yourself with everything you want to attract.

3. When finished, surround the rim of the lid with yellow wax and store it in a place where you will see it constantly.

65.   The Spell of Gold Wealth

Usage: This is a spell where you will imagine that you have all the gold in the world and that the world around you is golden like precious metal.

Ingredients:

- White salt
- Nutmeg
- Basil
- Parsley
- Cinnamon
- Tiger's eye crystal
- Clear quartz
- Golden candle
- Incense
- Jar

Procedure:

1. Light the golden candle and put yourself in meditation for a few minutes, where you imagine that you are surrounded by a lot of gold and that everything around you is golden.

2. Purify the jar that you imagine to be gold and begin to place each of the ingredients, which are also gold. Everything is gold.

3. When finished, seal it with gold wax and have the jar on your altar or in a representative place for you.

4. If you want, you can add a piece of paper where you can place messages of abundance inside.

66.   Green (But Not With Envy) Jar

Usage: Manifesting general success, prosperity, and power
Ingredients:

- A medium jar
- Salt
- Aventurine chips
- Jade chips
- Rosemary
- Spearmint
- Thyme
- Basil
- A mortar and pestle
- Cinnamon oil
- Green candle
- Incense of choice

Procedure:
1. Prepare yourself to cast the spell by meditating for at least 10 minutes.
2. Cleanse the jar and the mortar and pestle with incense.
3. Pour a generous amount of salt into your mortar. Add plenty of basil, spearmint, rosemary, and thyme. Grind them together with the salt.
4. Once the components are well-incorporated, add three drops of cinnamon oil and grind again until the oil is incorporated.
5. Pour this mixture into the jar. Top the mixture with layers of aventurine chips and jade chips.
6. Melt the green candle until the wax has formed a seal over the lid or cork of the jar. Add an additional green stone or green stone chips of your choice to the wax seal if you feel compelled. Leave this jar on your altar to invite power and success!

67. Make Success Stick Jar

Usage: To attract success and make it stick to you for a long time
Ingredients:
- A medium jar
- Molasses, maple syrup, or corn syrup
- A small piece of paper
- A pen/pencil
- Green candle
- Incense of choice

Procedure:
1. Prepare yourself to cast the spell by meditating for at least 10 minutes.

2. Cleanse the jar with incense.

3. Fill the jar to the top with the molasses or syrup of your choice.

4. On a small piece of paper, write down this mantra: "Success is stuck to me." Meditate over this paper and the mantra for as long as you need to.

5. Roll up the paper and stick it into the syrup. Stop up the bottle tightly and melt the green candle until the wax has formed a seal over the lid or cork of the jar. If you feel compelled, draw your own prosperity sigil into the wax. Keep this jar around to make success stick to you!

68. Fortune 500 Jar

Usage: Manifesting a prosperous life, promoting success quickly
Ingredients:

- A medium jar
- Salt
- Spearmint
- Jade
- Citrine
- A photo of someone successful who inspires you
- Orange candle
- Incense of choice

Procedure:

1. Prepare yourself to cast the spell by meditating for at least 10 minutes.

2. Cleanse the jar with incense.

3. Fill the jar halfway with salt. Sprinkle with spearmint.

4. Place one jade in the center over the photo of the person whose success you admire. Fill the jar the rest of the way with salt.

5. Melt the orange candle until the wax has formed a seal over the lid or cork of the jar. Put this jar under the full moon to charge, with a citrine resting on top.

Jar Spell Recipes To Attract Good Luck

69. To Banish Bad Luck

Usage: banishing bad luck
Ingredients:

- A medium-sized dark glass bottle with a cork;
- Lime tree;
- Three four-leaf clovers;
- A picture of you;
- Amber;
- Jasmine essential oil;
- Green candle for sealing

Procedure:

1. Insert the three four-leaf clovers into the bottle.
2. Add the linden leaf.
3. Add amber.
4. Add your photo folded in on itself.
5. Pour in a few drops of jasmine essential oil.
6. Cork the bottle and place it on a protected surface (a saucer, a box, or anything you don't mind ruining).
7. Light the green candle and wait for the wax to melt a little.
8. Being careful not to burn yourself, pour melted wax over the cap to seal your witch bottle.
9. Now your bottle is ready. Keep in mind that the auspicious day for fortune spells is Thursday, so, if possible, choose Thursday to other days to consecrate your fortune bottle. Bury the bottle.

70. To Be In The Right Place At The Right Time

Usage: Being in the right place at the right time.
Ingredients:

- A medium-sized dark glass bottle with a cork;
- Hypericum flowers;
- Four-leaf clover;
- Honey;

- Adventurine chips;
- Green candle for sealing.

Procedure:

1. Insert the honey into the bottle.
2. Add the four-leaf clover.
3. Add three flowers of St. John's Wort.
4. Add aventurine chips.
5. Cork the bottle and place it on a protected surface (a saucer, a box, anything you don't mind ruining).
6. Light the green candle and wait for the wax to melt a little.
7. Being careful not to burn yourself, pour melted wax over the cap to seal your witch bottle.
8. Now your bottle is ready. Keep in mind that the auspicious day for fortune spells is Thursday, so, if possible, prefer Thursday to other days to consecrate your fortune bottle. Bury the bottle.

71. To Stay Healthy All The Time

Usage: good health, ward off disease

Ingredients:

- A medium-sized dark glass bottle with a cork;
- Ash leaf;
- Four-leaf clover;
- Mandrake root;
- Nutmeg;
- A picture of you;
- Green candle for sealing.

Procedure:

1. Enter the nutmeg.
2. Add the four-leaf clover.
3. Add mandrake root;
4. Add the ash leaf.
5. Add your photo folded in on itself.
6. Cork the bottle and place it on a protected surface (a saucer, a box, anything you don't mind ruining).
7. Light the green candle and wait for the wax to melt a little.

8. Being careful not to burn yourself, pour melted wax over the cap to seal your witch bottle.

9. Now your bottle is ready. Keep in mind that the auspicious day for fortune spells is Thursday, so, if possible, prefer Thursday to other days to consecrate your fortune bottle. Bury the bottle.

72. To Make A Wish Come True

Usage: Fulfilling a wish
Ingredients:

- A medium-sized dark glass bottle with a cork;
- Beech leaf;
- Blueberry juice;
- Four-leaf clover;
- Carnelian chips;
- Pen and paper;
- Green candle for sealing

Procedure:

1. On a piece of paper describe the object of your desires. Roll it up and put it in the bottle.
2. Insert the beech leaf.
3. Add carnelian chips.
4. Add the four-leaf clover.
5. Pour in the blueberry juice until full.
6. Cork the bottle and place it on a protected surface (a saucer, a box, anything you don't mind ruining).
7. Light the green candle and wait for the wax to melt a little.
8. Being careful not to burn yourself, pour melted wax over the cap to seal your witch bottle.
9. Now your bottle is ready. Keep in mind that the auspicious day for fortune spells is Thursday, so, if possible, prefer Thursday to other days to consecrate your fortune bottle. Bury the bottle.

73. To Attract Luck In A Specific Area

Usage: Attracting luck in a specific area of your choice
Ingredients:

- A medium-sized dark glass bottle with a cork;

- Four-leaf clover;
- Violets;
- Carnelian chips;
- Pen and paper;
- Green candle for sealing

Procedure:

1. On a piece of paper, describe the object of your desires. Roll it up and put it in the bottle.
2. Insert violets.
3. Add carnelian chips.
4. Add the four-leaf clover.
5. Cork the bottle and place it on a protected surface (a saucer, a box, anything you don't mind ruining).
6. Light the green candle and wait for the wax to melt a little.
7. Becareful not to burn yourself and pour melted wax over the cap to seal your witch bottle.
8. Now your bottle is ready. Keep in mind that the auspicious day for fortune spells is Thursday, so, if possible, prefer Thursday to other days to consecrate your fortune bottle. Bury the bottle.

74. To Attract Luck In Love

Usage: Attracting luck in love

Ingredients:

- A medium-sized dark glass bottle with a cork;
- Red rose petals;
- Four-leaf clover;
- Poppy petals;
- Rose quartz;
- Rose water;
- Green candle for sealing

Procedure:

1. Insert the red rose petals.
2. Add poppy petals.
3. Add rose quartz.
4. Add the four-leaf clover.
5. Fill the bottle with rosewater.

6. Cork the bottle and place it on a protected surface (a saucer, a box, anything you don't mind ruining).

7. Light the green candle and wait for the wax to melt a little.

8. Being careful not to burn yourself, pour melted wax over the cap to seal your witch bottle.

9. Now your bottle is ready. Keep in mind that the auspicious day for fortune spells is Thursday, so, if possible, prefer Thursday to other days to consecrate your fortune bottle. Bury the bottle.

75. To Get Your Dream Job

Usage: Attracting good fortune in business

Ingredients:

- A medium-sized dark glass bottle with a cork;
- Pen and paper;
- Your resume;
- Four-leaf clover;
- Honey;
- Ginger;
- Green candle for sealing.

Procedure:

1. On a piece of paper, write down what your dream job or position is that you are applying for

2. Roll it up and put it in the bottle.

3. Add a copy of your resume to the bottle.

4. Add a tablespoon of honey and the ginger.

5. Add the four-leaf clover.

6. Cork the bottle and place it on a protected surface (a saucer, a box, anything you don't mind ruining).

7. Light the green candle and wait for the wax to melt a little.

8. Being careful not to burn yourself, pour melted wax over the cap to seal your witch bottle.

9. Now your bottle is ready. Keep in mind that the auspicious day for fortune spells is Thursday, so, if possible, prefer Thursday to other days to consecrate your fortune bottle. Bury the bottle.

76. To Attract Luck In The Lottery

Usage: Attracting luck to the lottery

Ingredients:

- A medium-sized dark glass bottle with a cork;
- 6 coins of your choice as long as the currency you need;
- A four-leaf clover;
- Pen and paper;
- Green candle for sealing

Procedure:

1. Insert coins into the bottle, one at a time, and for each coin, focus on the sound it makes when it falls to the bottom.
2. Write on the slip of paper the amount of money you wish to receive, then roll it up as if to form a small parchment.
3. Before you throw the parchment in the bottle, take a few minutes to think hard about the amount of money you intend to receive and how you would feel if you already got it;
4. Insert the four-leaf clover into the bottle;
5. Cork the bottle and place it on a protected surface (a saucer, box, or anything you don't mind ruining).
6. Light the green candle and wait for the wax to melt a little.
7. Being careful not to burn yourself, pour melted wax over the cap to seal your witch bottle.
8. Now your bottle is ready. Keep in mind that the auspicious day for fortune spells is Thursday, so, if possible, prefer Thursday to other days to consecrate your fortune bottle. Bury the bottle.

77. To Attract Luck In Sports

Usage: Attracting luck in sports

Ingredients:

- A medium-sized dark glass bottle with a cork;
- Cinnamon powder;
- Subject inherent to the sport played;
- Four-leaf clover;
- Aloe vera juice;
- Green candle for sealing.

Procedure:

1. Insert cinnamon powder;
2. Add the object inherent to your sport (ex: a tennis-a piece of a tennis ball).
3. Add the four-leaf clover.
4. Fill with aloe vera juice.
5. Cork the bottle and place it on a protected surface (a saucer, a box, anything you don't mind ruining).
6. Light the green candle and wait for the wax to melt a little.
7. Being careful not to burn yourself, pour melted wax over the cap to seal your witch bottle.
8. Now your bottle is ready. Keep in mind that the auspicious day for fortune spells is Thursday, so, if possible, prefer Thursday to other days to consecrate your fortune bottle. Bury the bottle.

78.   To Find A Lost Object

Usage: finding a lost object
Ingredients:

- A medium-sized dark glass bottle with a cork;
- Pen and paper;
- Four-leaf clover;
- Holly;
- Adventurine chips;
- Green candle for sealing

Procedure:
1. On a slip of paper, describe the lost item. Roll it up and put it in the bottle.
2. Add aventurine chips to the bottle;
3. Add the four-leaf clover to the bottle;
4. Add holly;
5. Cork the bottle and place it on a protected surface (a saucer, box, or anything you don't mind ruining).
6. Light the green candle and wait for the wax to melt a little.
7. Being careful not to burn yourself, pour melted wax over the cap to seal your witch bottle.
8. Now your bottle is ready. Keep in mind that the auspicious day for fortune spells is Thursday, so, if possible, prefer Thursday to other days to consecrate your fortune bottle. Bury the bottle.

79. For The Sex Of The Unborn Child

Usage: influencing the sex of the unborn child
Ingredients:

- A medium-sized dark glass bottle with a cork;
- Four-leaf clover;
- Blue or pink ribbon;
- Peach blossoms;
- Rhodonite;
- Green candle for sealing

Procedure:

1. On a piece of paper, describe the object of your desires. Roll it up and put it in the bottle.
2. Insert peach blossoms.
3. Add pink or blue ribbon.
4. Add rhodonite.
   Add the four-leaf clover.
5. Cork the bottle and place it on a protected surface (a saucer, a box, anything you don't mind ruining).
6. Light the green candle and wait for the wax to melt a little.
7. Being careful not to burn yourself, pour melted wax over the cap to seal your witch bottle.
8. Now your bottle is ready. Keep in mind that the auspicious day for fortune spells is Thursday, so, if possible, prefer Thursday to other days to consecrate your fortune bottle. Bury the bottle.

80. For Renewal Of Labor Contract

Usage: maintaining the workplace
Ingredients:

- A large dark glass bottle with a cork;
- A copy of your employment contract;
- Four-leaf clover;
- Honey;
- Poppy petals;
- Green candle for sealing

Procedure:

1. Print a copy of your employment contract. With a pen, change the contract end date (e.g., ~~2022~~ 2023). Fold it up and put it in the bottle.
2. Enter the four-leaf clover.
3. Add honey.
4. Add poppy petals.
5. Cork the bottle and place it on a protected surface (a saucer, a box, anything you don't mind ruining).
6. Light the green candle and wait for the wax to melt a little.
7. Being careful not to burn yourself, pour melted wax over the cap to seal your witch bottle.
8. Now your bottle is ready. Keep in mind that the auspicious day for fortune spells is Thursday, so, if possible, prefer Thursday to other days to consecrate your fortune bottle. Bury the bottle.

81. To Receive The Perfect Gift

Usage: Attracting good fortune in business

Ingredients:

- A large dark glass bottle with a cork;
- Four-leaf clover;
- Pen and paper;
- Dandelion honey;
- Carnelian chips;
- Green candle for sealing.

Procedure:

1. On a piece of paper, describe the object of your desires. Roll it up and put it in the bottle.
2. Add dandelion honey.
3. Add the four-leaf clover.
4. Add carnelian chips.
5. Cork the bottle and place it on a protected surface (a saucer, a box, or anything you don't mind ruining).
6. Light the green candle and wait for the wax to melt a little.
7. Being careful not to burn yourself, pour melted wax over the cap to seal your witch bottle.
8. Now your bottle is ready. Keep in mind that the auspicious day for fortune spells is Thursday, so, if possible, prefer Thursday to other days to consecrate your fortune bottle. Bury the bottle.

82. To Find The Car Of Your Dreams

Usage: finding the car of your dreams
Ingredients:

- A large dark glass bottle with a cork;
- Photos of your dream car;
- Four-leaf clover;
- Jasmine;
- Honey;
- Green candle for sealing

Procedure:

1. Insert a picture of your dream car into the bottle.
2. Add honey.
3. Add the four-leaf clover.
4. Add three jasmine flowers.
5. Cork the bottle and place it on a protected surface (a saucer, a box, or anything you don't mind ruining).
6. Light the green candle and wait for the wax to melt a little.
7. Being careful not to burn yourself, pour melted wax over the cap to seal your witch bottle.
8. Now your bottle is ready. Keep in mind that the auspicious day for fortune spells is Thursday, so, if possible, prefer Thursday to other days to consecrate your fortune bottle. Bury the bottle.

83. To Find Your Dream Home

Usage: Attracting your dream home
Ingredients:

- A large dark glass bottle with a cork;
- Photos of your dream home;
- Pen and paper;
- Four-leaf clover;
- Nutmeg;
- Honey;
- Green candle for sealing

Procedure:

1. Insert a picture of your dream house into the bottle.
2. On a piece of paper, describe your dream house in great detail. Fold it up and insert it into the bottle.
3. Add honey.
4. Add the four-leaf clover.
5. Add nutmeg.
6. Cork the bottle and place it on a protected surface (a saucer, a box, anything you don't mind ruining).
7. Light the green candle and wait for the wax to melt a little.
8. Being careful not to burn yourself, pour melted wax over the cap to seal your witch bottle.
9. Now your bottle is ready. Keep in mind that the auspicious day for fortune spells is Thursday, so, if possible, prefer Thursday to other days to consecrate your fortune bottle. Bury the bottle.

84.   To Always Have Good Luck

Usage: persistent luck

Ingredients:

- A large dark glass bottle with a cork;
- Cinnamon powder;
- Three four-leaf clovers;
- Three clovers;
- Yellow rose petals;
- Agate;
- Green candle for sealing

Procedure:

1. Insert the yellow rose petals into the bottle.
2. Add honey.
3. Add three four-leaf clovers.
4. Add three clovers.
5. Add cinnamon powder.
6. Insert agate.
7. Cork the bottle and place it on a protected surface (a saucer, a box, or anything you don't mind ruining).
8. Light the green candle and wait for the wax to melt a little.
9. Being careful not to burn yourself, pour melted wax over the cap to seal your witch bottle.

10. Now your bottle is ready. Keep in mind that the auspicious day for fortune spells is Thursday, so, if possible, prefer Thursday to other days to consecrate your fortune bottle. Bury the bottle.

85. For A Lucky Meeting

Usage: to foster a lucky encounter.
Ingredients:

- A medium-sized dark glass bottle with a cork;
- Four-leaf clover;
- Violets;
- Carnelian chips;
- Rose water;
- Green candle for sealing.

Procedure:

1. Insert the violets into the bottle.
2. Add the four-leaf clover.
3. Add carnelian chips.
4. Fill with rosewater.
5. Cork the bottle and place it on a protected surface (a saucer, a box, or anything you don't mind ruining).
6. Light the green candle and wait for the wax to melt a little.
7. Being careful not to burn yourself, pour melted wax over the cap to seal your witch bottle.
8. Now your bottle is ready. Keep in mind that the auspicious day for fortune spells is Thursday, so, if possible, prefer Thursday to other days to consecrate your fortune bottle. Bury the bottle.

86. To Always Arrive On Time

Usage: Always arrive on time.
Ingredients:

- A large, dark glass bottle with a cork;
- Pocket watch;
- Full moon water;
- Four-leaf clover;
- Daffodil flowers;
- Golden glitter.

- Green candle for sealing

Procedure:

1. Insert the pocket watch into the bottle.
2. Add the four-leaf clover.
3. Add daffodil flowers.
4. Add a handful of gold glitter.
5. Fill with moon water.
6. Cork the bottle and place it on a protected surface (a saucer, a box, or anything you don't mind ruining).
7. Light the green candle and wait for the wax to melt a little.
8. Being careful not to burn yourself, pour melted wax over the cap to seal your witch bottle.
9. Now your bottle is ready. Keep in mind that the auspicious day for fortune spells is Thursday, so, if possible, prefer Thursday to other days to consecrate your fortune bottle. Bury the bottle.

87. To Always Find Parking

Usage: finding parking on the first shot

Ingredients:

- A large, dark glass bottle with a cork;
- Hypericum flowers;
- Four-leaf clover;
- Pen and paper;
- Selenite chips;
- Green candle for sealing

Procedure:

1. On a slip of paper write "There is always a free parking space for me wherever I am. This is how I want it and this is how it will be." Roll it up and put it in the bottle.
2. Enter the flowers of St. John's Wort.
3. Add selenite chips.
4. Add the four-leaf clover.
5. Cork the bottle and place it on a protected surface (a saucer, a box, or anything you don't mind ruining).
6. Light the green candle and wait for the wax to melt a little.
7. Being careful not to burn yourself, pour melted wax over the cap to seal your witch bottle.

8. Now your bottle is ready. Keep in mind that the auspicious day for fortune spells is Thursday, so, if possible, prefer Thursday to other days to consecrate your fortune bottle. Bury the bottle.

88. To Bestow Good Fortune On Someone

Usage: finding someone who can help you

Ingredients:

- A large, dark glass bottle with a cork;
- Photo of the person;
- Acorn;
- Emerald;
- Three four-leaf clovers;
- Honey;
- Green candle for sealing

Procedure:

1. Take the photo of the person to whom you want to give good luck, roll it up and dip it in honey, then insert it into the bottle.
2. Insert acorn.
3. Add the emerald.
4. Add three four-leaf clovers.
5. Cork the bottle and place it on a protected surface (a saucer, a box, or anything you don't mind ruining).
6. Light the green candle and wait for the wax to melt a little.
7. Being careful not to burn yourself, pour melted wax over the cap to seal your witch bottle.
8. Now your bottle is ready. Keep in mind that the auspicious day for luck spells is Thursday, so, if possible, prefer Thursday to other days to consecrate your bottle of luck. Bury the bottle near the chosen person's house, unbeknownst to him or her.

Jar Spell Recipes For Physical And Spiritual Healing

89. To Heal Fast

Usage: If you have an illness, be it the flu or some minor illness, this spell will help you heal quickly.

Ingredients:

- Fennel seeds
- Calendula oil
- Amethyst
- Green candle
- Juniper berries
- Yerba santa
- Jar

Procedure:

1. Light the candle and purify the jar.
2. Meditate and imagine that you have all the health you seek. Meditate that you do not suffer from anything and that you are totally healthy.
3. Start placing the ingredients inside, one by one, while visualizing your good health.
4. Leave the oil last, seal it with green wax, and keep the jar with you until healed. Then throw it away and destroy the jar.

90. To Bring Health Into Your Life

Usage: If you want to have health yourself or yours all the time, this spell will be very useful.

Ingredients:

- Amethysts
- Bay leaves
- Coriander seeds
- Cinnamon
- Jamaican pepper
- Basil
- Chamomile

- Blue candle
- Jar

Procedure:

1. Light the candle and imagine that you have iron health; you can imagine yourself invincible, totally healthy, without even a pimple on your body.
2. Make the self-image of health and begin to purify the jar.
3. Place the ingredients and see that your intuition improves, and that your psychic abilities are more powerful.
4. When finished, seal it with wax and have it with you at home. Purify every new moon with spring water.

91. To Wish Someone Health

Usage: If a close person is sick, you can prepare this spell to make them feel better in no time.

Ingredients:

- Angelica root
- Blue witch salt
- White willow bark
- Rosemary
- Chamomile flowers
- Pumpkin seeds
- Elderflowers
- Vervain
- White candle
- Jar

Procedure:

1. Light the candle and purify the jar.
2. Begin a few-minute meditation as you imagine that the person is healed, in good physical shape, smiling, and glowing.
3. Place the ingredients with that image in mind. When finished, seal with white wax.
4. Give the person this spell as a gift or place it near where they are convalescing until healed, and then discard it.

92. For Inner Healing

Usage: If you feel that you have to heal something within yourself, you are overwhelmed by many situations, and you want something that science does not provide, this spell will help you.

Ingredients:

- Rosemary
- Sea salt
- Clear quartz
- Chamomile
- Nail
- Lavender
- Lavender oil
- Paper with intent
- Sky blue candle
- Jar

Procedure:

1. Light the candle and purify the jar.
2. Imagine that blue light enters you and begins to purify you completely. Imagine that it runs through you and cleanses you little by little.
3. While you do this, put all the ingredients in the jar.
4. When finished, seal it with blue wax and have it with you. It can be near your bed because while you sleep, you heal.

93. To Promote Good Health at Home

Usage: It is not only about you when we talk about health but about the whole family. This spell will help everyone to be always healthy.

Ingredients:

- Jar
- Incense
- Sage
- Spell oil
- Sigil
- Gray quartz crystal

Procedure:

1. Light the incense and purify the jar

2. Begin to meditate while thinking in your home. Imagine that a green light runs through it completely and goes through every corner, through each member of the house, healing them and removing all evil.
3. Place the ingredients inside and close.

94. To Heal Emotional Pain

Usage: If you have emotional pain, the kind that doesn't come out even when you cry deeply, this spell can help you heal.

Ingredients:

- Amethysts
- Bay leaf
- Coriander seeds
- Black pepper
- Basil
- Chamomile
- Cinnamon
- Jar
- Purple candle

Procedure:
1. Light the candle and begin to purify the jar.
2. Meditate while imagining that pain inside. You can see it inside. Imagine that evil as you want: something black, a bloody red ball, whatever you want.
3. Imagine a purple light attacking it as you place the ingredients inside.
4. In the end, seal and see that evil disappears and your body is totally healthy.
5. Keep the bottle close to you and discard it when healed.

95. To Heal Respiratory Diseases

Usage: If you have asthma, flu, or any respiratory disease, this spell can help you.

Ingredients:

- Coriander seed
- Eucalyptus
- Pyrite sand
- Nettle leaves
- Mint
- Tea tree oil

- Light green candle
- Jar

Procedure:

1. Light the candle and purify the jar as you begin to meditate.
2. Imagine your lungs full of mucus but a green light begins to cleanse them and make them healthy.
3. See your airways totally clear while you put the ingredients.
4. In the end, put a few drops of tea tree and seal with green wax.
5. If you can, place the jar close to your chest so you can heal faster.

96. To Maintain Physical and Mental Vitality

Usage: Whether you train or want to have vitality for the day-to-day, this spell can help you stay energetic and with the mental clarity that you want.

Ingredients:

- Jar
- Note of regeneration to the body
- Oak oil
- Rosemary
- Sage
- Vervain
- Rock crystal
- Aventurine
- Incense

Procedure:

1. Light the incense and purify the jar.
2. Imagine your body is totally healthy both inside and out. See that you have a lot of energy, calmness, and fullness.
3. Begin to place all the ingredients and leave the oil for the end.
4. Put the note inside and close.

97. To Relax the Mind of Bad Thoughts That Affect Health

Usage: If you have bad thoughts that affect your health, that don't make you feel good, I leave you this spell that will help you.

Ingredients:

- Black obsidian
- Pepper
- Rosemary
- Jar
- Cork
- Brown ribbon
- White candle

Procedure:

1. Light the candle and purify the jar.
2. Imagine your mind full of all the bad thoughts and how you are cleaning all that, purifying your mind.
3. Start putting all the ingredients into the jar.
4. When finished, seal it with the cork and place a loop around it. You can add white wax.

98. For Renewed Health

Usage: This is a powerful spell that will help you maintain iron health, as if you were 10 years old, with nothing wrong and a clear mind.

Ingredients:

- Snakeskin without hurting the animal
- Vegetable moss
- Red carnelian pearls
- Tourmaline beads
- Labradorite cabochon
- Jar
- Purple candle
- Sea salt

Procedure:

1. Light the purple candle and purify the jar.

2. Meditate while you think about the ingredients and their power, about the snake that is renewal and rebirth. Imagine that you renew yourself, that you leave your skin and cleanse yourself as a new person.
3. Put all the ingredients inside.
4. Seal the jar with wax and place it on the altar in a circle of sea salt.

99. Amulet for Health

Usage: Have this amulet with you to attract health all the time. You should carry it on your chest or in your hand, or wherever you want.

Ingredients:

- Pink salt
- Turmeric
- Cinnamon and rosemary
- Jar
- Brown bow
- Incense

Procedure:
1. Light the incense and purify the jar.
2. Imagine that amulet that will protect your entire body from the place where you will have it, that energy that comes out of there and protects you.
3. Place all the ingredients inside and meditate on your sanity.
4. Seal, accommodate, and carry with you always so that you have the protection you are looking for.

100. To Open The Mind And Spirit

Usage: You need to connect your spirit and your mind, and do deep and relaxing meditations that help you open your mind either to new knowledge or to change learned ways of thinking. This spell will help you.

Ingredients:

- Lilies
- Crystals that connect with you
- Nails
- Jar
- Black candle

Procedure:

1. Light the candle and purify the jar while you begin a meditation where you see the universe, immense and infinite, and colored lights that travel and land on you.
2. Start putting all the ingredients in the jar while looking open to new experiences.
3. Imagine that your mental blocks die and bury them with your nails.
4. Seal with black wax and bury in the back of your house or hide it.

101. For A Powerful Psychic Intuition

Usage: As a magician, you need to have your intuition open. This spell can help you.

Ingredients:

- Jar
- Sage
- Incense loaded in the new moon
- Spell oil
- Daisies
- Clear quartz

Procedure:

1. Light the incense and clean the jar. Place the stick where you want and start meditating while you put the ingredients inside.
2. Imagine and meditate now that you are with a deep mind and with your intuition on.
3. When finished, seal with a wax of the color of your choice.
4. Decorate with crystals and flowers.

102. To Clear the Spirit

Usage: If you feel a lot of restlessness and you feel bad, or your spirit seems to have no peace, this spell can help you.

Ingredients:

- Gray salt from Brittany
- Clear quartz
- White sage
- Opalite
- Moonstone
- Pink quartz
- Lemongrass
- Gold powder
- Icelandic moss dyed blue

- White candle
- Incense
- Jar

Procedure:

1. Purify the jar with the smoke of the incense first and then with the candle flame.
2. Visualize your spirit full of peace and calm, focused on what you want to see in it.
3. Begin to place all the ingredients inside while continuing to visualize each of the facts that you expect soon.
4. Seal with white wax.
5. You can take it with you or have it in your room.

103. To Believe In Your Own Magic

Usage: Maybe you think that your magic is not that powerful or you don't have the ability. Normally, you may doubt at first, but this spell will make you believe in yourself more.

Ingredients:

- Crystals that connect with you.
- Jar
- White roses
- Red roses
- Thyme
- Cilantro
- Incense
- Paper with affirmations
- White candle

Procedure:

1. Light the candle and purify the jar. Start repeating mantras where you support yourself and tell yourself that you believe in yourself.
2. Put the ingredients inside.
3. On the paper, write "I am blessed," "I am successful," and "I am a great magician."
4. Place it inside the jar, seal with white wax and keep it with you in a place where you will see it frequently.

104. To Increase Self-Esteem

Usage: If you feel that you lack self-esteem or want to strengthen it, this spell will help you greatly.

Ingredients:

- Clear quartz
- Dragon blood
- Incense
- Himalayan salt
- Lavender
- Paper with a self-love phrase
- Rose petals
- Pink candle

Procedure:

1. Light the pink candle and purify the jar while you think about all the love you have for yourself and what you can achieve.
2. Visualize yourself doing everything you don't out of fear and start filling the jar.
3. Light the incense and at the end, pass the smoke around the jar and repeat mantras that gives you strength to yourself.
4. Place the phrase of self-love that you want.
5. Seal with pink wax and have the bottle with you or in a visible place.

105. For The Blessing Of The Spring Spirit

Usage: The spirit of spring can protect you at all times and help you achieve what you set out to do. These are the steps to achieve it.

Ingredients:

- Mimosa
- Anemone
- Astrinance
- Amethyst chips, rose quartz, snow quartz, rock crystal, agate, and peridot
- Purple and white rope
- Incense
- Jar

Procedure:

1. Light the incense and begin the meditation process as you purify it.
2. Place the ingredients inside in the order you want.

3. When finished, seal and tie with the ropes in the way you want.
4. Close and place near where you pass most often.

106. To Increase Spiritual Energy

Usage: Spiritual energy is necessary for you to open your mind and feel better about yourself, so that you channel and can, for example, read the tarot with a broader vision. This spell will help you.

Ingredients:

- Eggshell
- Sea salt
- Dried rosemary leaf
- Lavender buds
- Chamomile
- Jasper chips
- Bracelet, earrings, or necklace
- Blue candle

Procedure:

1. Light the blue candle and imagine that the spiritual energy has fully expanded, and that you are an infinite being with a fully open mind.
2. Start putting all the ingredients in the jar while you meditate.
3. When finished, seal with blue wax.
4. As a recommendation, you can choose a small bottle, so you can always carry it in your pocket.

107. For Happiness

Usage: Be specific about the kind of happiness you want; happiness is not the same for everyone. After the vision is clear, the spell can begin.

Ingredients:

- Photo of a special day
- A scrap of old fabric or a favorite blanket
- Two crystals associated with happiness, such as peridot and citrine
- Wildflower petals
- Sweetgrass
- Incense
- Paper and pen
- Glass jar

Procedure:

1. Light the incense and purify the jar.
2. Clearly visualize the happiness you want and start placing each of the ingredients.
3. Write the intention and put it in the jar, remember to do it affirmatively.
4. Seal the jar with candle wax.
5. Place the jar where you will see it so that you remember that you are in the process of seeking happiness.

108. For Harmony of the Sun

Usage: The sun can bring you many benefits. One of them is to have harmony and peace around you. That's how you do it.

Ingredients:

- Himalayan salt
- Wormwood
- Rose petals
- Lavender
- Pink quartz
- Essential oil of rose and patchouli
- Jar
- Red candle

Procedure:

1. Light the candle and purify the jar.
2. Meditate while imagining that the sun caresses your skin with gentle heat and begins to fill you with good energy.
3. Place the ingredients inside one by one.
4. In the end, seal with red wax.
5. Keep the spell nearby and you can recharge it on full moon nights.

109. To Get Peace in the Street

Usage: When you go out, you need to have tranquility and harmony. Have this spell with you and you will see how you achieve it.

Ingredients:

- St. John's wort
- Damiana
- Mint
- Chamomile
- Lemon
- Ginger
- Orange
- Cinnamon
- Jasmine
- Carnelian chips
- White candle
- Jar

Procedure:

1. Light the candle and purify the jar.
2. Imagine that you are walking down the street. Visualize yourself outside, with peace, tranquility, and harmony. Nobody messes with you, everything flows with you.
3. Go fill the jar until it is complete.
4. Seal with white wax.
5. Have it with you in a bag. You can choose a small bottle so you can always carry it with you.

110. Pendant to Carry Tranquility Close to Your Chest

Usage: Have a pendant with you to always protect you wherever you go.

Ingredients:

- Citrine
- Lavender
- Dill seeds
- Altar salt
- Small jar with handle
- Pendant
- Incense

Procedure:

1. Light the incense and purify the jar.
2. Meditate imagining a light emerging from your chest and all around you.
3. Start putting all the ingredients inside while maintaining the meditation.
4. In the end, seal it, place it in the pendant, and take it with you whenever you want.

111. Earrings for Inner Harmony

Usage: You can take harmony with you wherever you want to go. For this, you will have to have these ingredients in fewer amounts.

Ingredients:

- Small jar earrings
- Soy wax
- Calendula
- Jasmine flowers
- Incense

Procedure:

1. Light the incense and purify the earrings.
2. Start placing the ingredients inside one by one.
3. Close and prepare the earrings.
4. Take them with you every time you go out or when you want to take protection with you.

112. Pocket Happiness

Usage: If you want, you can also take peace and happiness with you whenever you go out with this spell.

Ingredients:

- Citrine
- Juniper berries
- Small jar
- Cork
- Brown bow

Procedure:

1. This one contains only two powerful ingredients. Place in equal parts until full, close with a cork, and put a bow around it.
2. You can carry it in your pocket every time you go out.

113. For Happiness in the Workplace

Usage: Your work area should not lack peace and happiness. With this spell, you will attract it to your environment.

Ingredients:

- Chamomile
- Sunflower petals
- Roses
- Lemon oil
- White candle
- Jar

Procedure:

1. Light the candle and purify the jar.
2. Meditate about your work, the space where you work and how you feel, and the calm and fluidity in the whole place.
3. Place the ingredients inside.
4. In the end, seal with white wax.
5. Place it in your desk drawer or where you can see it.

114. For Inner Peace

Usage: If you want to have inner peace, this spell will help you.

Ingredients:

- White candle
- Black tourmaline
- Rosemary
- Pink salt
- Cedar
- Jar

Procedure:

1. Light the candle and purify the inside of the jar.
2. Do meditation and imagine peace as you see it. In this state of meditation and peace, begin to place all the ingredients.
3. In the end, seal it with white wax and have it in those spaces where you want there to be peace.

115. To Make A Gift Of Happiness

Usage: If you want to help a loved one to have peace and happiness, this is your spell.

Ingredients:

- Citrine
- Peridot
- Honeysuckle
- Chamomile
- Green candle
- Jar

Procedure:

1. Light the candle and purify the jar.
2. Meditate on seeing that loved one full of peace and tranquility, just as you want with that spell.
3. Fill the jar with the ingredients.
4. Seal with green wax.
5. Decorate as you like and give it as a gift to that special person.

116. To Make Your Presence Promote Happiness and Harmony

Usage: If you want your presence to generate harmony and peace wherever you go, you have to do this spell.

Ingredients:

- Himalayan pink salt
- Orange essential oil
- Calendula flowers
- Oregano
- Jar
- Yellow candle

Procedure:

1. Light the candle and purify the jar.
2. Start with a meditation where you imagine yourself being the center of attention, that people feel warmth when they see you and give them peace with your presence.
3. Place the ingredients, leaving the oils last.
4. Seal with yellow wax and keep it with you always.
5. As a tip, you can choose a small and portable bottle.

117. For Happy and Good Vibes in Complex Specific Situations

Usage: When there are complex situations full of tension, but instead you want to fill them with tranquility and soften them, this spell can help you.

Ingredients:

- Yellow tape
- Sage
- Lemon balm
- Sea salt
- Strawberry leaves
- Basil
- Cinnamon
- Mint
- Rosemary
- Yellow candle
- Jar

Procedure:

1. Light the candle and purify the jar.
2. Begin to meditate on the problem, visualize it completely, and now find a solution. Everything is fixed and calm.
3. Start placing the ingredients while imagining all the problems solved and the harmony around you.
4. Seal with yellow wax and place the jar in the area close to where the problem occurs.

118. To Increase Courage

Usage: If you need the courage to face any unforeseen event or new challenges, I leave you this spell.

Ingredients:

- Thyme
- Jar
- Purple candle
- Geranium flowers
- Black pepper
- Tiger's Eye

Procedure:

1. Light the candle and purify the jar.
2. Begin to meditate as you see yourself with more and more courage, full of great strength, and ready to face any challenge.
3. Place the ingredients one by one and seal them with purple wax.

119. To Multiply Inner Strength

Usage: Drive away negative forces and increase inner strength with this spell that will attract many positive things to you.

Ingredients:

- Protection oil
- Silver coins
- Licorice oil
- Rosemary
- Sage
- Jar
- Brown candle

Procedure:

1. Light the candle and purify the jar.
2. See your inner strength multiply until you become a powerful person.
3. Start to place the ingredients, leaving the oils last.
4. Seal with brown wax and let the candle burn to the end.
5. If you want, you can place it on the altar.

120. For Protection and Perseverance

Usage: To protect yourself and persevere in the face of any challenge you may face, this spell will help you.

Ingredients:

- Black tourmaline
- Turquoise
- Black obsidian
- Sage
- Artemis
- Jar
- Bee wax

Procedure:

1. Light the candle and purify the jar
2. Imagine in meditation that you have the strength and perseverance to be able to do what you set out to do. See yourself solving obstacles without giving up, always constant and persevering.
3. Place all the ingredients.
4. Seal and heat the beeswax.
5. Circle around and seal with the shape you want.
6. Have it close to you in those spaces where you want your life to improve.

Jar Spells Index

Conclusion

Witchcraft is a widely misunderstood craft; in the past, witches were accused of various demonic and terrible activities, which seemed to pique the interest of hundreds of people who imagined witches to be villains. It reappeared in the twentieth century, and it is frequently blamed for causing damage to property and people.

Witchcraft is thought to be the use of supernatural and magical forces to affect an individual, place, event, or property in either a good or bad way. Anthropological, theological, and historical settings are claimed to exist. It is widely regarded as "bad" or "dark," which is likely due to its role in several inexplicable events that happened throughout the twentieth century.

There's nothing wrong with studying to be a witch as long as you just aim to utilize it for non-harmful means and employ all of the talents you acquire in a practical and everyday setting.

Made in the USA
Monee, IL
10 July 2024